Online Learning and Assessment
in Higher Education

Online Learning and Assessment in Higher Education

A planning guide

ROBYN BENSON
AND
CHARLOTTE BRACK

Chandos Publishing

Oxford • Cambridge • New Delhi

Chandos Publishing
TBAC Business Centre
Avenue 4
Station Lane
Witney
Oxford OX28 4BN
UK
Tel: +44 (0) 1993 848726
Email: info@chandospublishing.com
www.chandospublishing.com

Chandos Publishing is an imprint of Woodhead Publishing Limited

Woodhead Publishing Limited
Abington Hall
Granta Park
Great Abington
Cambridge CB21 6AH
UK
www.woodheadpublishing.com

First published in 2010

ISBN:
978 1 84334 577 0
© R. Benson and C. Brack, 2010

Typeset by RefineCatch Limited, Bungay, Suffolk
Printed in the UK and the USA

Contents

Preface

Are you preoccupied with planning for tomorrow's lecture and the assignments that need to be graded by next week? Are you also vaguely aware that you could be using the online technologies available at your institution for a bit more than distributing PowerPoint slides or podcasts of your lectures? Perhaps you have no time and little inclination to even think about other online options you could pursue.

Or are you new to teaching, with a few hundred friends on your social networking site, fascinated by the use of microblogging to keep in touch, and excited about using online technologies for education? The possibilities might seem endless, but how do you merge what you know about learning and teaching with what your Head of Department requires and what you would like to explore? Maybe you are still working on your PhD, or have finished it and need to publish, and are pulled in too many different directions at the same time.

The speed at which new options for online teaching and assessing are emerging is breathtaking and the prospect of keeping up with them may seem overwhelming – and perhaps not worth the effort. One of the few certainties in the current higher education environment is that the tools available for extending the depth and breadth of teaching will continue to grow and diversify, underpinned by economic and social forces which impact on all major institutions, including universities. The extreme expectations associated with the promise of virtual universities have proved unrealistic but there has nevertheless been steady progress in the development of university policies, standards and infrastructure relating to online learning. The rate of progress is usually a few steps (or more) behind those who are pushing the boundaries of learning theory and practice to enhance online learning and assessment.

The latest opportunity and challenge to face university teachers interested in online learning has been the emergence of software that supports group interaction (Shirky, 2003). O'Reilly (2005) called this 'Web 2.0' to differentiate it from the static, non-interactive websites and proprietary rather than open source applications associated with Web 1.0.

This social software includes wikis, blogs, social bookmarking, social networking services, and virtual worlds. It has the potential of taking online pedagogy into largely uncharted territory, given the extent of online interaction between users, and between users and content, that it allows. At the same time it is important to remember that this is just the most recent manifestation of the evolution of online communication tools (Allen, 2004). While the technologies for engaging students online are developing, the principles underlying good teaching do not change with each new technological opportunity – the new tools simply provide new ways of implementing them.

Most teaching staff who have established some form of online presence in their teaching are likely to have used one of the proprietary learning management systems (also known as virtual learning environments) that emerged in the wake of the World Wide Web, with their array of easy-to-use and easy-to-assemble web-based tools. However, these systems are often used in a minimalist way for distributing information to students rather than for exploring and taking advantage of new ways of teaching. Their teaching and management emphasis can detract from a focus on the learner.

While some teachers are ready to seize the opportunities that online technologies offer, many reject them because of lack of interest, priorities in other areas (such as discipline-related research), adherence to conventional teaching methods, or lack of time. Increasing staff workloads and the time and commitment required for upskilling to understand and implement the possibilities available in technology-based learning environments are deterrents even when staff members would like to explore them. If you are interested in the potential of using technologies in your teaching or assessment, but have been discouraged for reasons such as these, this book provides a simple introductory framework to guide you.

Who is this book for?

This book is for you if you are looking for a quick and easy start to teaching online that is grounded in principles of good teaching practice from higher education. You don't even need to know too much about the technologies that are available to you, though whatever you do know will no doubt be helpful. We have assumed that you are responsible for teaching a particular subject or course and that you are working primarily as an individual, thinking about introducing technology into your teaching or assessment using systems and resources that are easily available to you.

You might identify with one of the two teachers profiled at the beginning or you may be somewhere in between. You are unlikely to be a technophile with specialised knowledge of online teaching who is already immersed in the use of new technologies. You might be undertaking a teaching qualification that includes online teaching as part of the course, or you could be teaching in areas other than higher education as the principles we cover transcend particular fields of education. Most of all, this book is for you if you are passionate about improving learning, have not yet explored the potential of the online environment for teaching and assessment, and are looking for a simple and practical way to take this step.

What is this book about?

The book is about the key points that you need to consider as a teacher if you are interested in using online teaching or assessment strategies to improve your students' learning. Although the selection and integration of technologies is part of this process, your planning needs to begin and end with educational considerations that may already be familiar to you.

In this book we aim to draw on some of the key ideas that are currently influencing the theory and practice of higher education, and combine these with some of the central ideas from the field of educational technology, to produce a simple and accessible planning framework for introducing online teaching and assessment which is focused on the needs of the learner. You do not need to be unnerved by the volatility of the educational technology landscape as the principles informing this framework are much less subject to change than the technologies themselves. Although the functionalities of emerging technologies offer different ways of interpreting these principles, and will certainly have implications for the way you teach, using them to guide your planning should remove any anxiety you might have about where and how you should start.

Structure of the book

To work through this planning process, the book is structured in the following way.

In Chapter 1 we ask you to think about your views of how students learn and we introduce two key learning theories that have influenced the fields of higher education and educational technology. We then ask you

to consider the nature of good teaching in higher education, the characteristics of your students, your characteristics as a teacher, and your learning and teaching context. This information, together with any particular issues or problems that you have experienced, or opportunities that you can envisage, which you think might be addressed by an online learning or assessment approach, will help you to identify the kinds of learning objectives that you will use to guide your planning. The contextual information and the objectives will allow you to determine the kinds of technologies that will be of most use to you. We then briefly consider the need to reconceptualise your teaching to suit the online environment. We conclude the chapter by summarising the key principles we have covered so far, and the main aspects of planning that you should have considered up to this point.

In Chapter 2 we focus on the technology options that are available to you. We begin by considering the affordances offered by various media and technologies and how these relate to different kinds of learning objectives. We then cover some of the main technology applications that you may be able to consider, including 'first generation' and subsequent internet technologies. We note the role of institutional policies and infrastructure in determining your options and the kinds of support, management and administrative issues that you may need to consider. You should then be able to decide on your options, building on the decisions you have already made at the end of Chapter 1. This ends your needs analysis. The next decisions you make will involve detailed planning for online learning design and development.

Pedagogical considerations will continue to drive the design and development decisions that you make in the context of the technologies you have chosen. In Chapter 3 we return to the objectives you have identified to determine the learning activities and the assessment tasks that you will design. We draw on some additional theoretical perspectives which may help you to conceptualise the individual and collaborative learning activities that you might include, and to inform the way that you structure learning activities, resources and support for your students. We also address feedback principles, options and issues which you will consider further in relation to assessment in Chapter 4. We then focus on integrating your design elements and note some key development issues which may influence your ability to implement your design. The chapter concludes by highlighting issues you may need to address in supporting students and in managing and administering online learning.

Chapter 4 begins by asking you to think about your reasons for assessment, taking a broad view of the nature of assessment, including its

formative and summative functions. We also ask you to think about who might have a role in assessing, particularly given the opportunities that the online environment offers for self, peer and group assessment, and assessment by others. We cover some basic assessment design principles, again grounding these in ideas about good practice in higher education. Then we focus on the main uses of the online environment for assessment, identifying some opportunities and challenges relating to each, and some of the key issues you may need to consider if you are assessing online. As in Chapter 3, we conclude by drawing your attention to issues you may need to address in supporting students and in managing and administering the online environment, in this case when it is used for assessment.

In Chapter 5 we introduce evaluation, although, in reality, evaluation needs to permeate all the previous stages. We consider some evaluation concepts, and suggest some ways that evaluation can be integrated during the design, development and implementation of your online environment, placing it in the context of quality control, and again drawing on theoretical principles and models from the fields of higher education and educational technology. We review some methods for evaluating online learning, teaching and assessment and then focus on the design of your evaluation plan, taking into consideration the purpose and audience of your evaluation and issues that you might need to address in managing, implementing, reporting and acting on the results.

Finally, in Chapter 6, we summarise the planning framework that we have built up over the previous chapters. We emphasise its appropriateness for accommodating new technologies, and new ways of teaching as they emerge, because it is built on pedagogical rather than technological foundations.

Acknowledgements

This book has been made possible by the generous permission of Monash University, copyright owner of material in the following chapters which we originally developed for academic professional development and teaching at the university. We acknowledge this permission with gratitude.

We are also enormously grateful to Dr Susan (Suzy) Edwards who has allowed us to incorporate her story about engaging with learning technologies in the book. Suzy is a Senior Lecturer in the Faculty of Education at Monash University. In less than seven years of teaching experience she has introduced major changes to her on-campus teaching through use of the online environment. She has won several university awards for excellence in teaching. In 2006 Suzy received a Citation for the design and implementation of innovative and reflective teaching practices in undergraduate teacher education from the Australian Learning and Teaching Council (ALTC) (then known as the Carrick Institute for Learning and Teaching in Higher Education), and in 2009 she won an ALTC Teaching Excellence Award in the early career category. She has led a project on reconceptualising learning and assessment at the University of New England (Australia) and recently completed a Visiting Research Fellowship in the Faculty of Educational Studies at the University of Oxford. While in the United Kingdom she also presented her work at the University of London (Institute of Education), the University of Exeter, the Open University (Milton Keynes) and Queen's University (Belfast).

In addition, we acknowledge the contribution of Monash University staff who have attended our workshops, used our resources and provided feedback on them, together with the work of previous staff members who were involved in the preparation of related materials. In particular, we recognise the contribution of Debbi Weaver, now of Swinburne University of Technology (Australia), to our recent series of workbooks on aspects of e-learning.

List of figures and tables

Figures

Tables

About the authors

Robyn Benson: I am a Senior Lecturer in Educational Design and e-Learning at Monash University, Australia. I have a MEd (Hons) in adult education and my PhD is in distance education. I have worked in educational design, development and research for over twenty years and during this time have undertaken and coordinated evaluation activities and programmes, developed and offered academic professional development programmes, and worked with teaching staff to increase the flexibility of their learning and teaching activities and resources. In recent years a particular focus of my work has been on the support of good teaching practice through the appropriate use of new learning technologies. As part of this I initiated the design and development of a series of 'workbooks' to support academic professional development workshops on aspects of teaching, and to act as standalone resources for staff. Recent workbooks have included an orientation to educational design and e-learning, and covered specific issues relating to online communication and online assessment.

Charlotte Brack: I am a Senior Lecturer in Educational Design and e-Learning at Monash University, Australia. I have an academic background in biochemistry with a PhD in protein structure and function from Melbourne University. I pursued research and teaching in the discipline and became increasingly involved in the challenges and theories of teaching and learning. I initiated and developed early computer-facilitated modules for teaching molecular mechanisms, moving to problem-based and online methods within the discipline. I subsequently moved into educational design more broadly and have since worked on innovations in learning and teaching across many faculties at Monash. A significant aspect of the successful implementation of innovations has been in providing professional development for teaching staff. To this end I have contributed to workbooks and workshops for academic staff. My educational design approaches in online environments revolve around situated learning, case and problem-based learning, experiential, authentic learning and using new technologies to support learning communities.

Where to start

Introduction

Where you need to start if you are thinking about introducing technology into your teaching or assessment is really in the same place that you would start if you were planning any new teaching activity. You need to think about how students learn and the nature of good teaching practice in higher education, in conjunction with:

- the characteristics of your students;
- your own characteristics as a teacher;
- the nature of the learning and teaching context; and
- the learning objectives (or learning outcomes) that you hope your students will achieve.

This information will inform your detailed planning.

In this chapter, we will begin by focusing on how students learn and the nature of good teaching practice as this will provide us with some generic principles about learning and teaching against which you can consider your own circumstances. These principles will also guide us as we reflect on issues related to online learning and assessment. We will be suggesting that the principles are relevant whatever the mode of learning, but that you nevertheless need to reconceptualise your teaching and assessment practices when you implement them online. We will consider why this is so towards the end of this chapter.

How students learn

How do you think students learn? How do you learn? Evidence from many lecture theatres around the world might suggest that learning is about students receiving knowledge from the lecturer. Indeed, as you are probably aware, during the mid-twentieth century, *behaviourism* was a dominant learning theory, with its roots in scientific positivism and the concept of the teacher passing objective truths to the student. This concept was very influential in the development of the field of educational technology. However, most currently accepted theories of learning in higher education suggest that learning is an *internal, intentional* change and that there are multiple ways of knowing. From this perspective, learning is not primarily about knowledge transmission and acquisition but, following Dewey and subsequent 'progressive' educators, involves the active engagement of learners in the experience of learning: 'It is not enough to insist upon the necessity of experience, nor even of activity in experience. Everything depends upon the *quality* of the experience which is had' (Dewey, 1963, p. 27).

In this tradition there have been two dominant learning theories in higher education in recent years. They are *phenomenography* and *constructivism*.[1] We will briefly outline these theories now, and will add a few more theoretical perspectives in Chapter 3. In this book we support the idea that learning is embedded in the student's experience but we take the view that, depending on your learners, your context, and the online approaches you might consider, it may be useful to have a few different theoretical lenses which might help you to conceptualise your learning design and the process of learning.

Phenomenography

Phenomenography arose from studies in the 1970s which identified 'deep' and 'surface' approaches to learning by students. It generated the field of study which came to be known as student learning research in higher education. It has been influential in the United Kingdom, Northern Europe and Australia but as Brew (2006) notes, it is virtually absent from American literature. According to this theory, the student's perspective is fundamental to the experience of learning: the world is not external and only exists through the student's eyes. The implication for teaching is that:

> ... [when] teachers mold experiences for their students with the aim of bringing about learning ... the essential feature is that *the teacher takes the part of the learner*, sees the experience through the learner's eyes, becomes aware of the experience through the learner's awareness. (Marton & Booth, 1997, p. 179)

While the curriculum is the same for all students in a unit of study, the way they will 'experience' and 'encounter' it and thus 'learn about' it may differ. In this context it is relevant to know about the characteristics of your students which describe how they learn. You can use this information to facilitate their learning.

Constructivism

As the name implies, from a constructivist viewpoint, learning is conceptualised as an active process in which learners construct new ideas or concepts based upon their own knowledge, both old (from the past) and new. Learning is seen as occurring best when it is *situated* in *authentic* contexts. Hence, problem-based and case-based learning are founded on constructivist ideas.

Constructivism has its basis in cognitive psychology. *Individual constructivism* refers to the construction of meaning by individual students while the idea of *social constructivism* is that meaning is constructed socially through the interactions that occur in a group. Constructivism became very influential in the American educational technology literature during the 1990s, highlighting the dichotomy between 'objectivist' (positivist) conceptions of learning associated with behaviourism, and constructivist perspectives focusing on the engagement of the learner in the learning experience (e.g., Jonassen, 1991; Duffy & Jonassen, 1992).

Table 1.1 from Oliver (2000), based on Grabinger (1996, p. 667), summarises the main differences between 'old' assumptions about learning and 'new' (constructivist) assumptions which focus on the *individual* processes involved in learning.

Developments in online learning have resulted in further support for ideas from social constructivism to explain how students learn as they engage with each other in the online environment. This concept is based on the theoretical perspectives of Vygotsky (1978) who focused on the social and dialogical aspects of internal development. He identified a *zone of proximal development* (which is the distance between the actual developmental level of a learner and the level of potential development as determined through the guidance of the teacher or collaboration with peers) and recognised the importance of support or *scaffolding* by the teacher until the learner becomes self-regulated and independent.

| Table 1.1 | Old versus new assumptions about learning |

Old assumptions	New assumptions
1. People transfer learning with ease by learning abstract and decontextualised concepts.	1. People transfer learning with difficulty needing both content and context learning.
2. Learners are receivers of knowledge.	2. Learners are active constructors of knowledge.
3. Learning is behaviouristic and involves the strengthening of stimulus and response.	3. Learning is cognitive and in a constant state of growth and evolution.
4. Learners are blank slates ready to be filled with knowledge.	4. Learners bring their own needs and experiences to learning situations.
5. Skills and knowledge are best acquired independent of context.	5. Skills and knowledge are best acquired within realistic contexts.
	6. Assessment must take more realistic and holistic forms.

Source: Adapted from Oliver, 2000, p. 19.

Comparing phenomenography and constructivism

An important distinction between phenomenography and constructivism relates to the view of the relationship between the learner and the environment. Phenomenography places emphasis on the learner, the object of learning, and other contributors to the experience of learning as a single entity, seen through the learner's eyes. It is therefore *non-dualistic*. In contrast, constructivism assumes that students are making meaning from a world that is *external* to them: there is a separation (duality) between the learner and an outside world. Richardson (1999, p. 67) notes that in 'focusing upon interindividual differences in conceptions, phenomenography appears unable to handle interindividual identity'. This may be one of the reasons that constructivism has been more influential in guiding thinking about online learning, especially its social aspects. However, phenomenography has also had an impact in guiding teaching with technology, particularly through the work of Laurillard (2002).

As Biggs and Tang (2007, p. 21) say, 'Whether you use phenomenography or constructivism ... may not matter too much, as long as your theory is consistent, understandable and works for you.' This also goes for other theories that we will consider later.

What is good teaching practice in higher education?

It is obvious that if you are able to articulate what you think learning is, and how students learn, as a teacher you will be trying to make that happen. Ramsden (2003) suggests that the aim of teaching is to make learning possible and that improving teaching is about understanding students' learning.

Chickering and Gamson (1987, p. 3) proposed a set of seven principles for good practice in undergraduate education which have become widely accepted as guidelines for improving learning and teaching in higher education. The seven principles state that good practice:

1. encourages contact between students and staff;

2. develops reciprocity and cooperation among students;

3. uses active learning techniques;

4. gives prompt feedback;

5. emphasises time on task;

6. communicates high expectations; and

7. respects diverse talents and ways of learning.

Ramsden (2003) suggests his own set of six principles which are about:

1. interest and explanation (making a subject interesting and helping students to make sense of the world, explaining why the material will be useful in the future);

2. concern and respect for students and student learning (being conscious and considerate of students, including being available to students, taking pleasure in teaching and developing a keen interest in what it takes to help them learn);

3. appropriate assessment and feedback (setting appropriate assessment tasks that demand evidence of understanding rather than just requiring students to rote-learn or reproduce detail, and giving helpful comments on students' work both assessed and non-assessed);

4. clear goals and intellectual challenge (explaining what must be learned in order to achieve understanding, and what can be left out for the time being, providing a clear structure focused on key concepts and keeping the challenge interesting);

5. independence, control and engagement (fostering a sense in students of choice over how to learn the subject matter, and control over what they focus on, providing tasks at the right level for students' current understanding, recognising that each student will learn best in their own way, and avoiding over-dependence); and

6. learning from students (constantly trying to find out the effects of your teaching on students' learning, and then modifying teaching in the light of the evidence collected).

You can see that there is overlap between the two sets of principles and that both focus on the experience of the student and the role of teaching in areas such as communication, guidance, giving feedback and nurturing the process of learning. This is very different from the idea of teaching as transmitting knowledge. As Ramsden (2003, p. 176) notes, drawing on the 'classic book' on assessment by Rowntree (1977), it indicates a need to get to know your students and the quality of their learning. The more you know about your students, the better your chances of being able to guide their learning.

What are the characteristics of your students?

With your ideas about the nature of student learning, and the characteristics of good teaching in mind, the next step, then, on the way to planning for online learning or assessment, is to take some time to consider the students in your target group – those to whom your efforts will be directed – and explore their world. Students cannot be regarded as a homogenous group.

There are four particular types of information about your students that may help you:

1. *Demographic:* information such as numbers, age range, occupations, employment, location, cultural factors.

2. *Motivation:* anticipated reasons that students will enrol, whether study is related to their work, what they hope to gain from it, etc.

3. *Learning factors:* such as level of study, prior level of general education, availability of time, facilities for study.

4. *Study background:* knowledge, skills, attitudes and personal experience of students which are relevant to this subject.[2]

Among the demographic factors that you consider, give particular thought to whether there are any predominant *generational* characteristics in your student group and, if so, whether they could have an impact on how you plan for online learning or assessment. There has been discussion in the educational technology literature about generational factors and preferences for learning with technologies. Cut-off dates for the differences between generations vary slightly between sources but, roughly, the generations include Baby Boomers (born 1946–64), Generation X (born 1965–80), Generation Y also called Millennials (born early 1980s – early 1990s) and Generation Z (born since the early 1990s). Prensky (2001) coined the terms 'digital natives' and 'digital immigrants' to describe these differences, suggesting that *'our Digital Immigrant instructors, who speak an outdated language (that of the pre-digital age), are struggling to teach a population that speaks an entirely new language'* (p. 2). However, others have suggested a need for caution in stereotyping students in this way. Bennett, Maton and Kervin (2008) review the evidence in the 'digital natives' debate and suggest that variation within generations is as great as between them. This is supported by a major Australian study which 'found little evidence that technology usage patterns can be explained primarily on the basis of broad generational differences – dispelling the digital natives versus digital immigrants argument' (Kennedy et al., 2009, p. 5).

Student diversity is another important issue which you need to consider, irrespective of the level of study. There will be differences within groups of students as well as between identifiable groups. You should be especially aware of the equity considerations raised by student diversity. These are some aspects of diversity which your group might include:

- students from non-English-speaking backgrounds;
- students from specific cultural or indigenous groups;
- students studying in a country other than your own;
- students from rural and isolated areas in your own country;
- students from socio-economically disadvantaged backgrounds;
- students who have a disability;
- women or men in non-traditional fields of study; and/or
- students who have been absent from the education system for a significant period of time.

> **For example ...**
>
> Depending on your teaching context, a particular issue you may need to address is the balance of local and international students whom you may be teaching, and whether the latter are studying on your local campus or in their home countries. Note any special arrangements you may need to make to meet the needs of these students – especially any access and equity issues that studying online might raise. These include availability of computers and internet bandwidth.

Considering the above factors will help you to pitch your material to suit the needs and interests of your learners. In addition, it will help with decisions in selecting examples and activities. You may not be able to gain all the information you need about your students but previous experience in teaching the subject will help. If you have not taught a particular student group before, it may be useful to talk to prospective students, lecturers or other staff who have close contact with students. You could also implement a diagnostic assessment activity at the beginning of your subject.

> **For example ...**
>
> If you have mature age students returning to study (even if they are actually quite young) you could use online learning strategies to determine their prior knowledge such as their level of familiarity with the subject or with educational technologies. Such diagnostic assessment could be done via a quiz which students complete prior to the start of their study. The knowledge gained would allow you to provide bridging material and appropriate support for those in need.

What are your characteristics as a teacher?

If you have been teaching in face-to-face settings for some time you will probably have a good idea of your characteristics as a teacher. You will know this from the feedback you receive from your students both informally in the way they respond to you and formally through student evaluations of your performance. You may also have information based on observations and reviews from your peers, and you will have valuable insights from your own reflections as you process all the information available to you, including your experiences and your perceptions of your qualities as a teacher.

If you are new to teaching you will have an idea of the personal qualities that you will bring to teaching and you will have gained relevant experiences through leading or talking to groups, or engaging in activities that are similar to teaching. You will also draw on your own experiences as a student to envisage the kind of teacher you hope to be.

Whether you are new to teaching or not, your views about learning and teaching will have a major impact on your characteristics as a teacher.

For example ...

- If you are an experienced lecturer you may have had feedback from students and peers that you engage and motivate students through your enthusiasm for your subject and your ability to involve students in it to support their learning. This would give you confidence that you are skilled at designing learning experiences that bring your subject to life for your students.

- If you are new to teaching you may rely on experiences of motivating others in your professional or personal life. You may have found that you are more comfortable with an informal collaborative style rather than a traditional lecture approach.

Thinking about teaching or assessing with technology adds another layer of characteristics about yourself that you will need to address. An interest in exploring the possibilities of learning with technology is probably the most important factor. Your familiarity with technologies and their use in your daily life will also have an impact. Through assessing your own skills in relation to teaching with technology you will be able to identify whether you need professional development, technical support or other assistance. Your institutional context is likely to provide the first indications of how you will access any support that you might need.

We will consider this more closely in Chapter 2. Working within the boundaries of the institution provides a supportive environment for you and your students. However, if your plans for online learning go beyond those boundaries you will need to assess the implications of being unsupported.

The learning and teaching context

The context of your students' learning and the context of your teaching may be markedly different, depending on whether you are teaching:

- only in a face-to-face context at a local campus or campuses;
- by combining your face-to-face teaching with online learning ('blended' learning);
- solely off-campus and/or online;
- in a transnational context; or
- across multiple contexts (for example, you may be teaching the same subject face-to-face, off-campus, locally and transnationally).

With the exception of online learning that is designed to be used during face-to-face teaching within the classroom or lecture theatre, all other online learning involves separation between teacher and learner, and probably between learners. This, in turn, means that your learners may be studying in a whole range of contexts, including home or work or fieldwork settings, or almost anywhere, given the possibilities of mobile learning. While you can't hope to accommodate all the contextual variables which will influence your students' learning, recognising this variation is important, along with identifying any particular contextual influences which may affect many of your students.

For example ...

- Some of your students may be studying in places where broadband internet access is not widely available. Downloading of large files would be problematic for these students. Therefore, using an online quiz for a timed summative assessment task that involved downloading of multiple images would not be a reasonable option.

- Considering the learning context may be particularly important if you are teaching transnationally so that you avoid making unrealistic assumptions about what you expect from your students. If a number of your students who are studying in a South East Asian country (with good internet access) are also in paid employment six days per week, it may not be reasonable to expect regular online discussion postings at short intervals.

Any contextual information that you have will be important in complementing what you know about the students themselves. Your institution will also have a dominant contextual influence on your students' learning, as well as on your teaching, because unless you are using a platform outside your university (in which case you will be on your own if problems arise), it is institutional policies, infrastructure, systems and standards, and perhaps further arrangements at faculty or department level, which determine the options available to you and the support you can provide for your students. We will consider this further in Chapter 2 in relation to selecting your technology options. Within the broad institutional framework in which you work you will also need to consider other contextual factors that may have a direct impact on your circumstances, as an online teacher, or on your students.

For example ...

- What support do you have (if any)? Tutors, markers, administrative support, technical support?
- Will others be teaching using materials you have designed (whether in a team teaching situation or separately)? If so, what perspectives about learning will they bring to the learning context and will they need professional development to implement your design?

You will need to consider this contextual information in conjunction with the student characteristics and your own characteristics as a teacher which you addressed earlier.

Identifying the learning objectives

Thinking about learning and teaching, students and teachers, and the context in which learning will happen, may feel like taking a very circuitous route to thinking about what your students will actually learn, but these things are important in setting the boundaries of any teaching episode. You are now ready to focus on the learning objectives that students will achieve by completing your course or subject. You may be familiar with the terms *learning objective* and *learning outcome*. We will be referring to both of these terms because the learning objective determines the intended learning outcome: the learning objective establishes the expectation of what the learning outcome will be, while the learning outcome does not actually occur until the learning has taken place. However, our main emphasis will be on learning objectives since these relate to the *planning* of learning and assessment which is our focus in this book.

A useful way to start, particularly if you are focusing on a subject that you have taught before, is to think about any issues or problems you have experienced that might be resolved by an online approach. Alternatively, you may be able to envisage some opportunities that online learning or assessment might offer. Then consider the learning objectives related to these issues, problems or opportunities and use them to guide your planning. If you have not taught the subject before, or if you are new to teaching, it is still important to think about your rationale for online teaching in terms of the relevant learning objectives.

The learning objectives should be at the centre of your planning because:

- achievement of them (or otherwise) will provide the evidence of whether the intended learning has occurred;

- they will guide the design of the learning activities that you plan to foster the learning of your students and also the assessment tasks that you set to identify whether or not they have been achieved;

- they will identify what 'content' you need to provide to help students to complete the learning activities and assessment tasks; and, importantly, if you are considering the use of learning technologies;

- they will play a key role in determining your technology options as we shall see in Chapter 2.

There is a skill to writing learning objectives well. In particular, they should:

- be *specific*, identifying exactly what students should be able to do to meet them; and
- require students to do something *measurable* or performance-based, so that someone other than the student can identify whether the objective has been achieved.

Try to avoid verbs like *understand* or *know* when writing cognitive learning objectives because they describe outcomes that are neither specific nor measurable.

It is interesting to note that although learning objectives (identifying specific, measurable behaviours) were associated with behavioural psychology concepts of the mid-twentieth century, they have transcended the developments in understandings about learning which have occurred since then and are applicable to perspectives of learning which focus on the experience of the learner. Hence the importance of their role has been supported from a phenomenographical perspective (e.g., Laurillard, 2002) and from a constructivist perspective (e.g., Biggs & Tang, 2007).

The scope of a learning objective can vary, with broader subject-level objectives supported by narrower, more specific objectives for components of the subject. At an even broader level, the extent to which students can meet particular learning objectives may be used to determine whether they have accomplished identified *graduate attributes*. These are the desirable characteristics, skills, abilities and learning achievements which students take with them when they leave their course. Ideally, they are reflected in objectives at all levels.

There are a number of tools available to assist you in developing learning objectives. One way to do this is to use the taxonomy of educational objectives developed by Bloom and his colleagues in 1956 and revised by Anderson et al. (2001). This taxonomy identifies six categories in the cognitive process dimension from the simple recall or recognition of facts, through to increasingly complex and abstract cognitive processes, as shown in Figure 1.1.

Verbs to identify behaviour for each cognitive process can then be used in the writing of objectives (see Table 1.2). You will find many examples of verbs for writing learning objectives if you search the internet. Table 1.2 provides a sample list.

Figure 1.1   Bloom's (revised) taxonomy of educational objectives

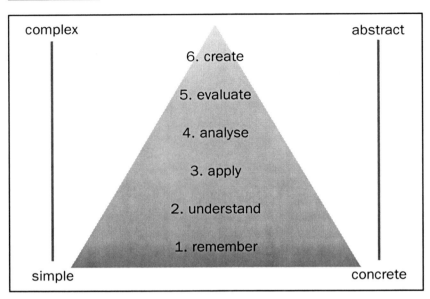

complex   abstract

6. create

5. evaluate

4. analyse

3. apply

2. understand

1. remember

simple   concrete

Table 1.2   Verbs for writing learning objectives using Bloom's (revised) taxonomy

	Cognitive process dimension	Verbs for writing learning objectives
1.	Remember	arrange, define, duplicate, label, list, memorise, name, order, recall, recognise, relate, repeat, reproduce, state
2.	Understand	classify, describe, discuss, explain, express, identify, indicate, locate, recognise, report, restate, review, select, translate
3.	Apply	apply, choose, demonstrate, dramatise, employ, illustrate, interpret, operate, practise, schedule, sketch, solve, use
4.	Analyse	analyse, appraise, calculate, categorise, compare, contrast, criticise, differentiate, discriminate, distinguish, examine, test
5.	Evaluate	appraise, argue, assess, choose, compare, defend, estimate, evaluate, justify, judge, predict, prioritise, rate, select, support
6.	Create	arrange, assemble, collect, compose, construct, create, design, develop, formulate, manage, organise, plan, prepare, propose, set up

> **Please note:**
>
> - While Figure 1.1 is organised to show the lowest cognitive levels at the base of the diagram, with the highest at the top, Table 1.2 moves from the lowest levels at the beginning of the table to the highest levels at the end.
> - Anderson et al. (2001) also identify four knowledge types associated with each cognitive process (factual knowledge, conceptual knowledge, procedural knowledge and meta-cognitive knowledge). The examples of verbs in Table 1.2 have not been classified into these knowledge types.

Learning outcomes from level 1 represent the remembering of previously learned material, and are generally recognised as the simplest level of learning outcomes. As students move up the levels of the pyramid, their ability to critically analyse new material, solve problems and propose innovative solutions increases. Usually, in supporting learning, we aim to assist students in moving up these learning levels.

Reconceptualising your teaching

What we have covered so far has suggested that to prepare for online learning and assessment you need to start in exactly the same place that you would begin the planning of any teaching episode. We support this view strongly. As Ramsden (2003) states, the principles of good teaching do not alter when information technology is used appropriately to help make learning possible. However, we do not want you to think that this means that you should teach online in exactly the same way as you do in a face-to-face setting.

> **For example ...**
>
> If your strength as a teacher is currently based on your expertise in your subject and your teaching style on a traditional lecture format, then it may seem that recording your lectures to put them online would be an appropriate strategy for transforming your

teaching to an online mode. This allows you to offer your expert knowledge to students at any time or place if they have access to the internet. However, when students listen to (or watch) your lecture online you have no feedback from them and no way of knowing how they are receiving the information and the extent to which it is contributing to their learning. You would be continuing with a transmission-of-content approach to teaching which you have found successful in a face-to-face context. You may consider that students will respond in the same way as they do in the lecture theatre but that is rarely the case.

The assumption that teaching occurs in the same way irrespective of the medium is often the biggest mistake that beginning online teachers make. Note the following comment by Laurillard (2008, p. 139):

> [T]he solutions technology brings, in their most immediate form, are solutions to problems education does not have. The current vogue for podcasting ... is an excellent solution to the problem of providing personalised mobile auditory wallpaper. However, no one ever suggested that the reason why education is failing is that learners do not have enough access to people talking to them.

So what is the same and what is different?

The key point here is that current perspectives about learning in the fields of higher education and educational technology may be seen as reflecting the same kinds of belief systems, values and epistemological assumptions. Both draw on perspectives, common to a number of contemporary learning theories, which support the contextual, negotiated nature of knowledge, and the centrality of the learner's experiences. Despite differences in the dominance of particular theories within each field, the underpinning principles are similar, though we need to acknowledge that theories and principles do change over time, as has occurred with the movement from behaviourism to constructivism. It is the way these principles are implemented in the online environment that may involve a major reconceptualisation of how you teach.

The changes in your teaching will occur as a result of the functionalities of the technologies you choose which will offer ways of doing things that are not possible or are more cumbersome in the face-to-face environment. As we have said elsewhere, in relation to recent developments in learning technologies:

> ... the capacities of Web 2.0 technologies to facilitate collaborative learning through social software such as blogs and wikis and access to virtual worlds (O'Reilly, 2005) has changed the way learners can retrieve, share and evaluate information, and create knowledge. Hence, these technologies have enabled a flourishing of person–person and person–content interactivity, changing the mechanisms of interactivity and introducing possibilities for learning that have yet to be fully explored and which lend themselves to new ways of investigating how learning occurs. (Benson & Brack, 2009, p. 74)

We will consider some of these capacities in Chapter 2. Our main purpose in asking you to begin to think about this now is to reinforce the point, before we get to thinking in detail about the technologies themselves, that simply using the online environment to replicate what you do in the lecture theatre is a wasted pedagogical opportunity (though it may offer some advantages in terms of convenience for students).

Illustrating the ideas in this chapter ...

The story that follows describes how one lecturer (Suzy) has considered the kinds of factors that we have covered in this chapter, in order to prepare for teaching online.

Suzy's story

I lecture in early childhood education. I am committed to individual and social constructivist ideas about how learning occurs and I use problem-based learning principles to guide my teaching. Thus, my view of good teaching is to encourage students to become actively involved with the problem that they will solve, the issues relating to it, and the theoretical content that informs it. My role is to embed the unit content in these problems, and to support students as they address them. They also support each other in working together, whatever their backgrounds.

My students have diverse backgrounds. They range from Generation Y to mature-age students and they have varying prior experiences with the online environment. They are all studying on-campus but I find the learning and teaching context frustrating! I feel locked in by the on-campus teaching model which allows for a one hour lecture and a one hour tutorial per week. I know that technology allows you to do things differently and I would like more freedom to explore this. I have tried to be innovative in my teaching which has been recognised by awards I have received. However, I'm definitely not highly computer literate. I aim to work with technological tools provided by the university, using the institutional and faculty support that is available, and seeking further support when I need it.

I'm particularly conscious of the importance of encouraging practice that has a sound theoretical basis. I've been intrigued by the double standards of lecturers who lecture on the topic of constructivism to a theatre full of bored and disengaged students, rather than supporting students in constructing meaning themselves. Therefore, in one of the units that I teach, I was keen to develop an online learning approach that would allow students to *apply* theory to practice as they met the following objectives. In this unit, students are required to:

- identify and discuss the key issues in relation to infant and toddler care and education programmes; and
- critically examine the literature on infant and toddler childcare and be able to relate the findings to their own experiences with infant and toddler programmes.

I wanted to design an assessment task that would enable the pre-service teachers, working in groups, to develop an understanding of how theory could be used to frame their conceptions of quality care and teaching with young children. To do this, students would need to create a practical (although fictional) context for the content they were engaging with through the readings and lectures. I decided to ask them to prepare a series of digital responses to complete this task. I knew that this would involve a major reconceptualisation of how I taught the unit.

Summary

This chapter has covered some of the important factors that you will need to address if you are thinking about embarking on online teaching or assessment. You might respond to some of these factors intuitively, perhaps based on years of teaching practice, but there may be value in thinking things through consciously, given the implications that the online environment offers for major changes in the way you plan your teaching. There may be additional factors that you think you might need to consider to prepare for introducing these changes, and you should note these as well.

Following is a checklist that summarises the main planning stages we have covered in this chapter. We will extend it in each of the following chapters in order to develop a complete, introductory planning framework by the end of the book. However, in doing this we do not want to suggest that introducing online learning and assessment is as simple as ticking boxes. Your planning will only be as good as the thinking behind each of your responses, and you may not address each point in the same order as we present them.

Nevertheless, you might find this useful to trigger your thinking about factors related to learning and teaching as you begin to explore the online environment. If you are able to answer 'Yes' to most questions, you are probably ready to start, even though you might be unsure about some things. If your answer to most questions is 'No' it could be worthwhile speaking to a few people in your institution who have been identified as champions of online teaching, or exploring the academic professional development options that are available to you, or connecting with a professional association that supports teaching with technology in your area. You could consider attending a conference or reading a few academic papers about online teaching that may be relevant to you.

Are you able to identify ...	Yes	Unsure	No
1. Your views on how your students learn (preferably as they relate to one or more contemporary learning theories)?			
2. Your position in relation to current views about the nature of good teaching in higher education?			

Are you able to identify ...	Yes	Unsure	No
3. The characteristics of your students that may be important for online learning or assessment?			
4. Your characteristics as a teacher that may be important for online teaching or assessment?			
5. Aspects of both the learning context and your teaching context that may be important for online teaching or assessment?			
6. An issue, problem or opportunity related to the learning or assessment of your students that allows you to recognise one or more learning objectives that they may be able to meet online?			
7. How the transition to online learning or assessment may require you to reconceptualise your teaching?			
8. Any other factors that may encourage you to consider online learning or assessment? (Specify below.)			

Notes

1. There are many other theories that may help you to conceptualise aspects of learning, including online learning. We have focused on phenomenography and constructivism because of their major influence on the fields of education we are concerned with in this book.

2. We use the word *subject* to refer to a unit of study (usually over a term or semester), which together with other subjects contributes to a *course*, with successful completion of the course resulting in the award of a diploma or degree (e.g., Bachelor of Arts; Master of Economics).

2

Teaching with technology – considering your options

Introduction

The technology options that are appropriate to meet your needs and those of your students will be determined largely by the factors you considered in Chapter 1, even though most of them may have appeared to have little to do with technology. With these factors in mind, in this chapter we will work through some of the main issues that you need to consider in identifying your options, with a view to making a final decision about the technologies that will meet your needs by the end of the chapter.

We will begin with your learning objectives. As we have already suggested in Chapter 1, these play an important role in the selection of technologies because what your students need to do to meet the objectives has to be matched with technologies that offer the functionalities you require. If you are planning to use technology infrastructure provided by your institution (which we have suggested is advisable if you are new to online teaching in order to ensure institutional support), this is another key issue that you will need to think about which may influence your options.

We will consider the above two issues before focusing on the technologies themselves and outlining some of the main online tools that are currently being used for learning and assessment. We will then briefly address what the future might hold. What you are able to select from these options will also be determined by further student support, management and administrative issues. We will cover some of these additional issues. They are likely to narrow your options even further.

Once you have made all these decisions, it should be fairly clear what your technology options are. How you use them will then be determined by the design and development decisions you make which we address in Chapter 3. This will involve the idea of reconceptualising your teaching which we introduced in Chapter 1.

Technology affordances and learning outcomes

Laurillard (2002) popularised the use of the term *affordances* in relation to educational technology to describe the support for various kinds of learning experiences which are offered by different kinds of media. Bates (2005) provides a useful distinction between the terms *media* and *technology*. He suggests that a *medium* is a generic form of communication associated with particular ways of representing knowledge, and that each medium may use several different delivery *technologies*. What this means if educational technology is to be used, is that an intended learning outcome, as specified by a learning objective, will require the selection of a medium and technology with the properties that will allow that objective to be met.

> ## For example ...
>
> If an objective is that students will be able to 'discuss the advantages and disadvantages of using Wikipedia for research', then you would need to use a medium (and a related technology) that allows discussion to occur. Using a presentational medium such as audio would obviously not be suitable (though discussions can be recorded and presented in this way).

Laurillard (2002, p. 90) identified five media forms, relating them to examples of methods or technologies used to deliver them and the kinds of learning experiences that they support. In Table 2.1 we have updated her explanation to include examples of Web 2.0 applications which are now available to extend learning experiences relating to all media forms. (Note that Laurillard uses the term 'interactive' to refer to interaction with presentational media where users can navigate and select content. Later we use it more broadly to refer to relationships between users, as well as between users and content, and users and the computer interface.)

The implications of this approach are that you should examine the kinds of learning experiences students will need to have, based on the learning objectives that you have identified, and then select technologies

Table 2.1	Five principal media forms with the learning experiences they support and some examples of methods used to deliver them

Learning experience	Method/technologies		Media forms
	Laurillard's examples	Additional Web 2.0 examples	
Attending, apprehending	Print, TV, video, DVD	Podcasts, iTunes, YouTube	Narrative
Investigating, exploring	Library, CD, DVD, web resources	Social bookmarking	Interactive
Discussing, debating	Seminar, online conference	Social networking sites	Communicative
Experimenting, practising	Laboratory, field trip, simulation	Virtual worlds (e.g., Second Life)	Adaptive
Articulating, expressing	Essay, product, animation, model	Blogs, wikis	Productive

Source: Adapted from Laurillard, 2002, p. 90.

within an appropriate media form that will allow students to have these experiences and meet the objectives.

One of the issues you will need to think about when you consider technology affordances and learning outcomes is that narrative technologies offer passive, rather than active, learning experiences. However, they can certainly be used to trigger active learning. Alternatively, the use of narrative technologies *by students* to generate content themselves can provide a valuable active learning experience for them that could form part of their assessment. Web 2.0 applications, in particular, lend themselves to this due to their facility for the creation of content online.

Now that you have an idea of how the learning objectives begin to shape your choices of the technologies that will be appropriate for you to use, we will consider how the policies and infrastructure of your institution may further influence your choices.

Institutional policy and infrastructure

There is usually a time lag between the availability of new technologies and their uptake by universities (Barnes & Tynan, 2007). The technology infrastructure offered by your institution for teaching and learning will encompass technologies available for your use which have achieved a state of 'sustainable embedding' (Nichols, 2008). It is generally best to use these technologies if you are new to online teaching because, not only will there be support in cases of technology failure, it is also likely that your institution will offer associated professional development for staff, as well as support for students. In addition, software that links the technology to your institution's student administration system means that your students can log in without difficulty, and security and privacy issues are also addressed: you are not exposing students' details and contributions to a private provider or an environment available to the public. A further important aspect is that if you are primarily interested in issues of learning and teaching and, in relation to technology are not necessarily an 'innovator' or 'early adopter' (Rogers, 2003), this allows you to focus on the pedagogy and avoid the frustrations of dealing with technology breakdowns, or administrative tasks such as manually enrolling students into non-institutional systems. Your institution may have policies on these matters that limit or preclude the use of external software or providers.

If a state of sustainability in relation to particular learning and teaching technologies has been achieved by your institution, a number of prior processes will have occurred. It will mean that formal strategic planning by your institution has encompassed adoption of these technologies, informed by appropriate academic leadership. This will have led to the implementation of institutional policies related to the technologies, and accompanying standards, systems and procedures. Your institution's central information technology service will have taken responsibility for implementation of appropriate hardware and software, including backup and support procedures. The decision-making and costs involved in ensuring appropriate institutional provision contribute to the time lag mentioned above. This is often related to ensuring that particular technological innovations have matured sufficiently so that the advantages to learning and teaching are clear and warrant the investment involved. Many institutions have adopted proprietary learning management systems/virtual learning environments (LMSs/VLEs)[1] to provide an aspect of infrastructure and a set of tools designed for online teaching and learning. These systems are continually evolving, although they are also characterised by the same institutional time lag in the incorporation of new technologies.

While using your institution's chosen platform will limit your technology choices and your ability to take advantage of cutting-edge innovations in technologies, it will also mean that you are likely to be introducing online teaching or assessment approaches in a secure environment where advantages to learning have already been established. There are usually still plenty of innovative opportunities that you could explore in the ways that these technologies might be used. Use of your institutional system will not preclude you from incorporating innovations beyond the system in the future.

Keep the issues that we have just considered in mind as we now provide an overview of some of the technologies available for learning and assessment. Focus on those that appear to be most relevant for you based on your learning objectives and institutional context. We will then ask you to consider some further student support, management and administrative issues towards the end of the chapter.

The evolution of internet technologies for learning and assessment

Tim Berners-Lee began development of the World Wide Web in 1989 but it was not until the Mosaic web browser became available in 1993 that the internet became widely accessible (Richardson, 2009). The development of Web 2.0 applications followed the dot-com collapse in 2001: before this the web was characterised by static, non-interactive websites and proprietary rather than open source applications (O'Reilly, 2005). Nevertheless, the social potential of the online environment for education was being explored prior to, and in parallel with, these developments, with an acceleration in the use of computer mediated communication in the 1980s (e.g., Mason & Kaye, 1989) reflecting the evolution of social software which Allen (2004) suggests began in the 1940s.

In this and the following sections, we will consider the affordances of various technologies in three main categories: those that allow interaction between users; those that involve interaction with content; and a third subsequent category which combines aspects of the other two, accommodating interaction between users and with content, allowing creation of content by users. We also add a fourth category for other forms of interaction not included above.

Following the development of the World Wide Web, the major coordinated development that supported both interactive and content-based options for online learning and assessment in higher education was the emergence of proprietary learning management systems as mentioned earlier. These systems brought together a range of tools that teachers could select from, manage themselves and use within a single online learning environment. They are prevalent in universities around the world and new tools continue to be developed for them, or to be available as 'plug-ins', though there is now also considerable competition from open source systems. It is quite possible that when you select your technology options, you might be choosing from the tools available within your institution's learning management system.

The most recent developments within the World Wide Web have followed the advent of Web 2.0 applications. Web 2.0 refers to the different ways that software developers use the web rather than to any change in technical specifications. The significant differences relate to ways that information is shared, the interoperability of software, and the ways in which communication is set up, with the term 'social software' used to describe applications which facilitate online communities. Before venturing into using these for teaching and learning it is wise to understand how 'first generation' internet technologies, which are part of these new options, work.

The term 'first generation' in relation to technologies refers to fundamental capacities of the internet which allow interaction between users and with content. We will consider these at a basic level before exploring the ways in which new technologies, including social software, use and extend them.

Choosing your technologies is a first step in planning your online learning environment once your pedagogical requirements have been identified. In the next two sections we will look at some first generation technologies that you might consider for online learning or assessment. In Chapter 3 we will address some important design issues to consider once you have chosen your technologies.

We will consider interactive options first because these are directly related to active learning. Interactivity in relation to computer based applications has been interpreted in many ways. In the context of online learning, Sims (1999) refers to interactivity as a form of human–computer dialogue, where the user initiates action and the computer responds. Sims includes in this description computer feedback to a learner response (which he refers to as adaptation), participation with the computer software as in a 'game', and communication with other users. We will include options that allow interaction between users, between user and content, and between user and the interface. We will begin with interaction between users. If your objectives require communication, this is usually one of the easiest ways to introduce online interaction.

First generation internet technologies: options for interaction

Interaction between users

Common online communication tools used in higher education for interaction between users include email, asynchronous discussion and text-based (synchronous) chat. Email is the most common form of asynchronous online communication. It can be used to support one-to-one or one-to-many interaction, and also to convey information in the body of the message (including links to websites) or via attachments. In the context of online learning and assessment it is particularly valuable for private communication but is cumbersome for communication between groups, which is where asynchronous discussion groups (or bulletin boards) offer advantages. These can be used for individual communication within a group and for a range of group activities, including debates, case-based learning, role plays, and project-based collaboration. We will consider some of these options in Chapter 3. The ability to 'thread' messages on the same topic is an important organising feature. They can also be used for support and community building and for access to 'guest lecturers' and other experts, as well as to you. Alternatively, synchronous text-based online chat offers the advantages of real-time communication and this can contribute significantly to a sense of identity and the building of an online community.

These forms of communication have benefits for teaching but they also have limitations, an awareness of which will help you to choose your tools wisely. While asynchronicity places management of communication in the hands of the receiver, thereby enhancing the flexibility of online learning, the time delay can be frustrating for a sender who is hoping for an immediate response (such as a student requiring clarification in order to complete a learning activity). Online chat allows real-time communication but requires everyone to be available at the time specified and can be cumbersome to manage as the conversation is often disjointed as comments are keyed in and posted. Nevertheless, for those who are available to participate, online chat provides an important point of contact. Transcripts of a conversation can be circulated for the benefit of those who could not take part. Table 2.2 summarises some of the benefits and limitations of email, asynchronous discussion and synchronous chat.

| Table 2.2 | Some specific benefits and limitations of communication tools | |

Tool	Specific benefits	Limitations
Email	■ Seamless integration of learning and teaching activity with other email activities. ■ Record of conversation is visible to all. ■ Communication can occur at convenient times. ■ Attachment of files allows sharing.	■ Mixes up learning and teaching activity with other email activities which makes following a thread difficult. ■ Managing groups is more cumbersome.
Asynchronous discussion	■ Separates learning and teaching activity from other work activities. ■ Threaded record of conversation is easily viewed, reviewed and followed. ■ Communication can occur at convenient times. ■ Attachment of files allows sharing. ■ Lends itself to group management.	■ Teachers and learners have to go specifically to the discussion space. ■ Contributions can be missed when activity in the discussion space is sporadic.
Synchronous text chat	■ Creates an online 'community' with a sense of belonging (particularly useful for off-campus learners). ■ Record of interactions can be saved.	■ Requires scheduling (for participants to be available at the same time) which reduces flexibility. ■ Technology is cumbersome, requiring fast typing; participants tend to leave the session if their entry to the space is not acknowledged immediately. ■ Conversation is often disjointed because of different typing speeds. ■ Does not allow sharing of files.

Figure 2.1 Using online discussion to explore a case study

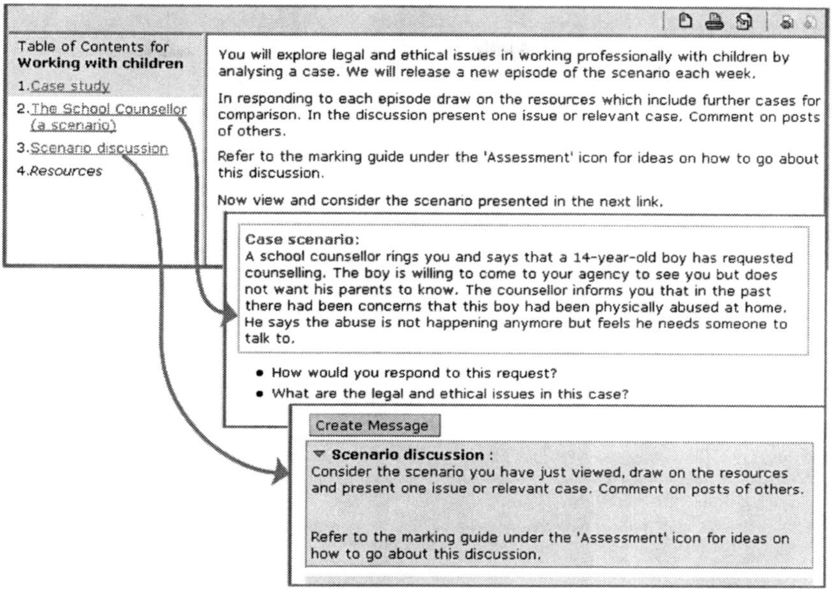

The value of these tools for learning or assessment is dependent on the ways in which they are used. Students don't discuss spontaneously; they need explicit tasks and support. This can be given via the discussion itself or can be built into the surrounding environment as illustrated in Figure 2.1 which provides an example of how online discussion can be used for case-based learning.

Figure 2.2 shows a chat session within an LMS, indicating the layout (interface design) and the nature of the text space.

We will explore issues relating to online design for interaction between users in Chapter 3.

Interaction with content

One of the main advantages that web-based resources offer over linear, narrative technologies such as video and audio is the ability to navigate, search for and select content. This may allow students to meet objectives that require exploration of resources but it may not be sufficient to guarantee effective learning.

Figure 2.2 The layout and nature of a chat session

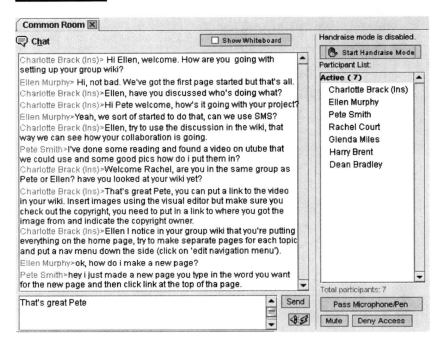

For example ...

Teaching staff often express concern about students who use an internet search engine for a literature review, rather than appropriate databases related to their discipline, and who do not recognise the differences in the quality of what they might find.

Students may need to be supported in developing academic literacy by exploring the differences in ways of searching for information.

Did you know...?

Library databases use keywords chosen by authors, information related to the publication (title, author, journal, publisher, etc.) and subject identifiers as metadata for retrieval purposes. Internet search engines also use metadata but they use a 'web crawler' to follow every link and algorithms to analyse the contents of pages and determine how a page should be 'indexed' so it can be retrieved for later search queries. The index is stored in a database which is interrogated by the search engine. Different search engines use different algorithms so they index and store data differently: some use the whole source code of a page, others use only parts of pages, and they choose different criteria to rank pages. Whereas the library database only stores particular types of information (e.g., published, peer-reviewed), internet search indices store data on all web pages.

Other forms of interaction

Other common forms of interaction include quizzes and surveys, and multimedia interactions that may be designed to include automatic feedback. There are many tools readily available for the former (for example, within an LMS) but the development of multimedia interactions is usually costly, involving the skills of a multimedia developer and a complex design and development process. During the 1990s the proliferation of software programs resulted in many multimedia 'packages' which created interactive environments for self-directed offline learning. These programs use media which are external to the tools of an LMS but they can be used as components within it (embedded) or linked. They can also be used within Web 2.0 environments such as wikis or blogs.

Figure 2.3 illustrates an online quiz using a tool within an LMS to help students meet knowledge-based objectives.

Figure 2.4 also illustrates a quiz which is designed to help students meet a knowledge-based objective, using a multimedia interaction rather than an LMS quiz tool. This provides more flexibility in the way that an item, and the feedback on it, can be presented but it requires the specialist technical skills of a multimedia developer to prepare. An activity may be constructed entirely in a multimedia format, or may be a hybrid of multimedia and html (the language used for web pages). The advantage of the latter is that the html component is easily modified over time. Elements constructed by multimedia developers are usually exported in formats viewable in a web browser but are not themselves editable. Any change to the activity requires further input from the developer. While these are often

Figure 2.3   Using automated feedback for learning in an online quiz

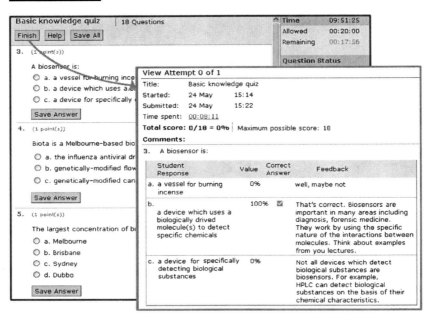

still relevant they are limited by their inflexibility when it comes to amending them. If specialised technical skills are required you may need to explore funding options before you start development and you would need to allow additional time. For your first experience of setting up an online learning environment it is probably best to focus on learning objectives that students will be able to meet using tools that are already available which you can set up yourself (with some support, if necessary).

In Figure 2.4, the multimedia software allows the consequences of the student decision to be explored in an animation which gives feedback to reinforce learning.

First generation internet technologies: options for managing content

If your objectives indicate that you need to prepare content for your students so that they can complete a task, you have a number of choices of the format you might use in an online environment. These choices

Figure 2.4 A multimedia application with automated feedback

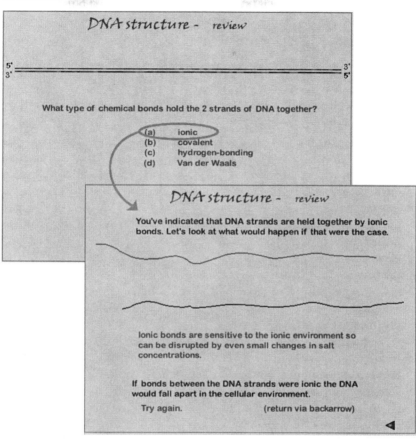

include: text (e.g., Word document, pdf, html), presentation software (e.g., PowerPoint), audio, video, animation (e.g., Flash), images and graphics (e.g., gif, png, jpg), etc. The choice of media and the design of the content depend on the objective of presenting it to students. We will explore here some of the issues involved in presenting content in different ways.

- **Text-based content:** Whether or not you need to develop text-based content for your online sites will depend on your target audience and their access to libraries or other resources. Often adding vast amounts of content online is not the most efficient way for students to learn (how many of us still prefer to print out material to read?). If your students have easy access to printed material such as printed study guides, textbooks and journal articles, then you don't need to add this online. Instead, you can focus on developing content that is best provided via electronic media, for example, animations, audio or video segments.

If you do add content as text to your online site, writing for online delivery is quite different from writing for print. For instance, good online writing is often less formally structured, and includes fewer words but more explanation.

- **Visual content:** The online environment allows you to communicate content in other ways so that you can capitalise on the features of the electronic medium and address different learning styles. For instance, visual learners will benefit from content interpreted visually. Images, graphics, animation and video can, in some cases, communicate an idea or concept more efficiently than words. This is evident in documentaries such as *Walking with Dinosaurs*. Here, not only the viewers were enlightened but the scientists also found they learned an enormous amount from having to visualise beings and events. Video and images can communicate context which is not immediately available to the learner. Obviously, video is a good choice for film and theatre studies.

  Animations created by multimedia developers are an effective way of visually illustrating a concept or process involving movement, and these can easily be included in an online environment. If you are considering animations as an option (which will involve the costs and complexities of multimedia development) you should search first to see if a suitable example already exists as a reusable learning object. Many textbooks now have associated online learning centres which include animations that are accessible to the public.

  Graphics such as diagrams, concept maps and mind maps can convey concepts and relationships between ideas. They can be used for navigation purposes, although introducing into an LMS a level of navigation that conflicts with the system's navigation can be confusing. There are several software programs available for concept mapping. You could use one of these to develop comprehensive and informative maps.

- **Aural content:** An audio file can be useful when voice-based content, including tone of voice, is important or when you need to personalise learning. An audio with an image of the speaker can be used to introduce a subject or topic. The image provides additional information to students about the speaker. Audio files can also be used to convey real life sounds such as heart sounds and breathing patterns, and have use in music or in pronunciation for language learning.

- **Media databases:** Your LMS may include a tool which allows you to develop a database of media items or terms such as a glossary or image library. Generally, students access items as required by clicking on hyperlinks in a list or table, which is located together with other resources for that topic. In addition, throughout the unit, hyperlinks to individual items can be automatically created whenever the name of the particular item occurs (you can control whether you want this to happen or not).

* * *

Table 2.3 summarises some issues and questions you should consider when you are planning the provision of online content for your students.

If you want your students to view a video, large image files, or multimedia applications, the online environment may not be appropriate. These may be more easily viewed by students on a CD-ROM or DVD so that download time (bandwidth) is not an issue.

We will now move on to Web 2.0 and other recent internet applications so that you can think about how students might be able to meet additional kinds of objectives using these tools, or perhaps meet objectives you have considered in relation to the above options in more efficient or effective ways.

Web 2.0 and other new options for interaction

Web 2.0 environments are all about interaction and creation of content, and divisions between opportunities for interaction and opportunities for managing content become blurred. The technologies for managing content on the web remain largely the same (e.g., text, images, audio, video) but there is a dramatic increase in the way content may be produced, managed and shared, particularly in the context of interaction between users. Examples of Web 2.0 applications include social networking sites, image or video-sharing sites, blogs, wikis, mashups and folksonomies. These terms are described in Table 2.4.

| **Table 2.3** | Content development – some issues and questions |

Text-based content (Word, pdf, html)

- Documents in Word and pdf formats will generally have to be downloaded from your site by students, whereas html files are accessible on the web server. This means that html files are easier for the user to view, but they are harder for you to produce (unless you are adept at it already, of course).

Presentation format

- Students often ask for PowerPoint files online. Remember that PowerPoint was designed to support face-to-face presentation. You can record a narration synchronised with the slides in full-screen mode.
- Many institutions have recording facilities for podcasting audio or video files of lectures. As with all elements of your site, ask yourself if it would disadvantage your students if the file was not online.

Visual content

- Images: images downloaded from the internet need copyright clearance. Only use them if it is necessary and therefore worth contacting the copyright owner, and/or paying the required fee. There are many banks of images available online; make sure you read the fine print.
- Graphics: there are many drawing and mapping programs available, or you can scan any hand drawn graphics.

Audio/video content

- What do the aural and visual elements add to this form of content? If the visual aspect of a video doesn't carry any important message about context, or doesn't help to visualise an environment, then you may be able to dispense with it and have a still image with an audio. This has benefits in terms of bandwidth: videos are usually larger than audio files and take longer to download.
- You will need a quiet place to record.
- Audio and video need to be kept as short as possible; think about your own tolerance levels. For this reason it is often wise to write a script.

Table 2.4 indicates a range of options, some of which you may choose to use when you are familiar with working in online environments for teaching. The ways in which creation and manipulation of content occur are highly significant in terms of learning and teaching due to the implications for shared production online, and the opportunities for facilitating collaborative processes. Therefore, in this section, we will look at the affordances relating to interaction between users and interaction with content again.

Table 2.4 Recent technologies – some terms, definitions and examples

Term	Definition/description	Examples/applications
Blog (Weblog)	Online journals or diaries typically 'owned' by individuals, with comments contributed by others	Sharing information and ideas
Folksonomy	Collaborative creation and management of tags to annotate and categorise content. Tags (metadata) are generated by users (social tagging), not only by experts (as in search engines)	Aggregating the tags of many users creates a folksonomy, e.g., Delicious
Web hosting service	Used to share specific content, connect with 'like' content	Image and video-sharing, online photo/video management and sharing applications, e.g. Picasa, Flickr, YouTube
Mashup	Digital media file containing any or all of text, graphics, audio, video, and animation, which recombines and modifies existing digital works to create a derivative work	Student projects
Mobile learning	Learning that takes advantage of mobile (portable) devices	*Mobile phones:* Text messaging (Short Message Service) to facilitate communication between lecturer and students *Tablet computers:* used in lectures or tutorials to enhance communication between teacher and students
Podcast	Audio/video which is syndicated, i.e. delivered via an RSS feed over the internet to a subscriber. Requires a host server	Content online; students create a site and connect with similar sites

(Continued)

| **Table 2.4** | Recent technologies – some terms, definitions and examples (*cont'd*) |

Term	Definition/description	Examples/ applications
Shared documents	Non-html documents which are editable online	Google Documents for word processing, spreadsheets, presentation and forms
Social software	Software which facilitates social interactions. Defining activities: conversational interaction, social feedback, and social networks	Social networking sites of which Facebook is just one example. There are many different social networking sites each with different characteristics
Virtual worlds	Online simulations such as those used in 'the Sims' type of computer games	Active Worlds, Second Life
Web 2.0	Web development and design that facilitates communication, secure information sharing, interoperability, and collaboration on the World Wide Web	Web 2.0 concepts have led to the development and evolution of web-based communities, hosted services, and applications such as social-networking sites, video-sharing sites, wikis, blogs, and folksonomies
Wiki	Editable webpage 'owned' by groups	Wikipedia

Interaction between users

The proliferation of web-based social networking sites has highlighted the potential of Web 2.0 applications for communication and collaboration. Some use of the large privately-owned social networking sites is also being made for education, but you should think carefully about using these sites for teaching, taking into consideration issues such as:

- ownership of the information emerging from a learning–teaching interaction;
- your lack of control in that environment, relating to factors such as privacy, copyright, plagiarism, security of the data, and of your students; and
- lack of integration with your institution's administrative systems.

On the other hand, use of students' 'owned' lines of communication (e.g., Facebook, SMS, Twitter) facilitates learning in ways which learners control and this encourages them to take responsibility for their learning and enhances their independence. However, they may not necessarily recognise the potential for learning of communication tools that they use for other purposes (Kennedy et al., 2009) and there is evidence that they may not appreciate intrusion on their social spaces (e.g., Sharples, 2007).

We will now cover some of the tools that may be available on institutional servers which allow interaction between users. We will begin by considering the nature of blogs and wikis and provide an overview of how they might be used for online learning or assessment, and then look at some of the other Web 2.0 communication tools.

Blogs

A blog (weblog) is a website where users can post contributions and comment on contributions or comments of others. Posts can be text or images and can include video or audio files. They are dated and presented in reverse chronological order (new ones appear at the top). They can be archived so that if a blog lasts a long time posts are categorised by date. Blogs are usually about making content freely available to anyone, getting your voice heard, and generating discussion around your area of interest. This may be in a global context or it can be limited to a smaller group of users.

A blog can be:

- a personal one where only one person can post and those invited to participate can comment (this works well for a journalling or reflective activity);
- personal for posting but open to all for comments;
- a group blog where several people can post and only those invited can comment; or
- a group blog where all can comment.

Table 2.5 summarises the configuration options.

For the purposes of learning in higher education, a blog might be used as a limited forum so that it can meet specific needs in a specific time, or it might be fully open if 'authentic' public responses are important in the context of the related learning objective/s. Blogs are particularly useful in allowing students to meet learning objectives that require them to reflect and record their responses. Blogs can facilitate online discussion of

Table 2.5 Configuring a blog

Blog configurations	Who can add new postings?	Who can comment on existing posts?
Fully closed	Owner only	Invitees only
Closed post ('normal')	Owner only	Anyone
Invited post ('group blogs')	Invitees only	Invitees only
	Invitees only	Anyone
Fully open	Anyone	Anyone

Figure 2.5 Example of a blog used for a student project

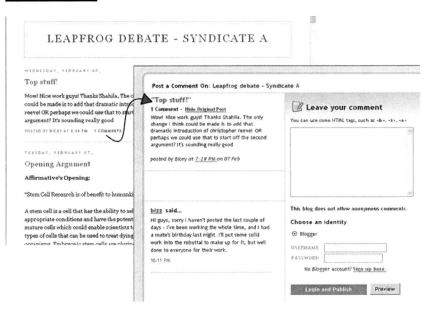

subject material as they can display both the material for discussion and the discussion thread itself on the same screen. See Figure 2.5 for an example.

Wikis

The word *wiki* is derived from the Hawaiian 'wikiwiki' meaning 'quickly'. A wiki is a website which enables users to add to, edit and delete from the

Table 2.6   Open, protected and private wikis

Access	Open	Protected		Private
Edit	Open to all	Members only	Members only	Members only
Comment	Open to all	Open to all	Members only	Members only
View	Open to all	Open to all	Open to all	Members only

site's content *quickly*. It incorporates a *discussion space* and a *history* for each wiki 'page'. The history is a chronological list of all the changes that have been made to the page together with the identity of the editor. Previous versions of the page can be viewed and restored (if the changes are deleted).

Table 2.6 shows the different access levels that are available for managing wikis.

How can wikis be used in learning and teaching? In a face-to-face context, the output of group work is often a presentation supported with PowerPoint slides. When the group work cannot be accomplished or completed in 'class' time, preparing the PowerPoint file becomes cumbersome. The file must be sent between group members, introducing problems of time delay and version control. Further, the PowerPoint file format is designed to support a presentation rather than a standalone output, and there is no indication of collaborative inputs. Wikis address these issues and provide a number of advantages for group work.

Wikis are useful for student group work because the degree of collaboration can be monitored through the discussion and the contributions of individuals can be observed through the discussion and history. For the history to be informative the editing must be done using the wiki editor. A disadvantage of wikis at present is that the web editing is limited to text and images. However, the web editors used for wikis are increasingly complex and today's limitations will be gone tomorrow. Wikis enable students to work online collaboratively on a single group output. The output (the wiki pages) stays on the wiki server so students do not have to download files, work on them and upload again. This gives students greater flexibility in group work as it alleviates the pressure to meet face-to-face.

Figure 2.6 shows an example of a wiki created by students as a group project. Students were given the task of diagnosing a medical problem,

Figure 2.6 The homepage of a student group project wiki

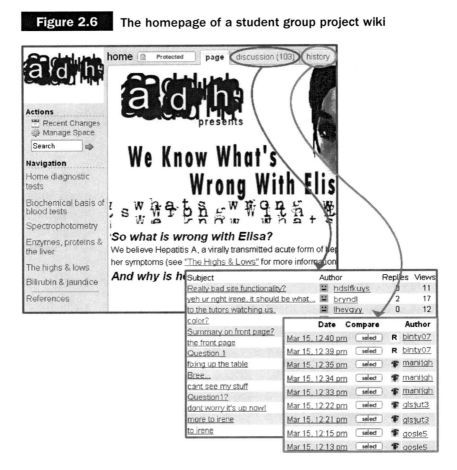

via a case study called 'What's wrong with Elisa?' Resources were accessible in an LMS site and each group developed their analysis of the case in their group wiki. In this example the students have set up their wiki with links to sections in a navigation menu on the left. In the discussion associated with the homepage students negotiated the site construction, the content they were including in the site and project management issues such as division of labour, timelines and evaluation. The history allowed teachers to assess the contributions of students and track the development of the site by comparing versions of each page. In assessing the group project students were told that careful construction and editing would attract more credit than importing large blocks of text which might raise suspicions about plagiarism.

Shared documents

There are numerous applications for sharing web-based documents. Proprietary applications have extensive functionality for online collaboration (often used in research), but freeware is also available. The most popular application is Google Documents which allows web-based word processing, spreadsheet, presentation and form applications. This enables users to work on a shared document that remains on the server, which is useful for group work when the output required is in one of these formats. The focus of the technology is on the document and collaboration through discussion is not specifically facilitated.

Online videoconferencing and web conferencing

Online (PC) videoconferencing offers the potential of real-time communication that is much less cumbersome than text-based chat. Through online videoconferencing you can set up meetings with or between students and have some of the benefits of face-to-face interactions online. However, to take full advantage of the technology, users must have the client software installed and have a headset, microphone and a video cam. The client software is freely available, while the server software required to set up the 'meetings' requires a licence which may be available through your institution. Web conferencing (which allows all users to see the same screen at the same time in their web browsers) and online videoconferencing may be enhanced by other tools, including file sharing capabilities, whiteboards, chat programs and polling. Web conferencing may be used for purposes such as real-time meetings, presentations, demonstrations or 'webinars'.

Mobile technologies and interaction

Mobile devices applicable to interaction for learning and assessment include laptop and handheld computers, portable digital voice recorders and, especially, mobile phones. At an institutional level, mobile phones are increasingly used to contact students on administrative issues such as enrolment, timetabling, venue changes, and notifying results using SMS (Short Message Service). Their use for learning is growing and applications include communication with and between students on placements or field trips.

Internet messaging such as MSN (Microsoft) can also be used to communicate with students and for students to communicate between themselves. This is more successful if students already use these technologies in daily life. These tools can be particularly useful for students collaborating in groups. They allow them to arrange meetings (virtual or real), divide tasks, etc. Skype is free software which allows users to make free calls over the internet to any other user who also has Skype. While this is mostly for two way communication, the technology can be used to hold a meeting of several people.

Electronic audience response systems can be useful in a lecture for diagnostic testing and engaging students. Tablet computers are increasingly used for this purpose. These allow input of data using a stylus or 'digital pen' on a touch screen, which can be combined with use of the keyboard for communication between users. They facilitate engagement and learning by students who can annotate online or prepare hand-drawn diagrams and communicate with the lecturer directly. The lecturer can then share selected contributions with the whole class.

Interaction with content ... and other users

In addition to the interaction with content allowed by first generation internet technologies, Web 2.0 applications facilitate interaction with content in sophisticated ways which can combine with interaction between users. There are many examples of this type of interaction but it is exemplified in online role playing games described as 'massively multiplayer online role playing games' (MMORPG) in which a very large number of players interact with one another within a virtual world.

Games, simulations and virtual worlds

While social software facilitates communication between users and with content which is largely determined by and controlled by the user, gaming software is designed to facilitate interactions which, at least to some extent, are controlled by the software designer. Gaming software is used for a wide range of simulation software designed for learning and teaching. The development of such software has flourished in the area of technical instruction, resulting in sophisticated software in industry such as the flight simulator. Games such as those from the Sims franchise (e.g., SimCity) were developed for the commercial market and originally pre-dated Web 2.0 applications. However, use of the newer technologies facilitates and extends the development and implementation of software based on a 'game' metaphor.

If some of your objectives require experience-based learning, Web 2.0 applications which support games, simulations and virtual worlds with immersive, collaborative engagement through designed experiences (Squire, 2006) may be relevant. Authentic challenges are presented in narrative social spaces, requiring the collective action of the players (Amory, 2007). Reeves, Malone and O'Driscoll (2008, p. 64) note the benefits for life and work of merging real and virtual worlds (for example, 'online games can be informal but realistic simulators for contemporary leadership training' that is immediately applicable in business).

In Table 2.4 we listed two examples of virtual worlds (Active Worlds and Second Life) which are commonly used in education, but there are dozens of platforms available. Integration of virtual worlds with learning management systems is in progress but the time and expertise required to create the world and then work within it make it a high risk choice for learning, particularly if you have not taught in the online environment before.

While some of these environments are widely used socially as web-based multiplayer role playing games, their uses for learning are still limited. If you are considering role playing as a learning activity, and are new to online teaching, it may be best to begin to explore your ideas using pre-Web 2.0 applications initially (such as role playing in online discussion groups). While less exciting, this will allow you to clarify your educational strategies and gain experience before applying these ideas with more complex technologies.

Web 2.0 and other new options for managing content

One of the key advantages of Web 2.0 applications is the ease with which they allow development and sharing of content (both visual and textual) by users. While delivery of content by the teacher is not precluded, your main emphasis in relation to content if you are considering the use of Web 2.0 applications may be on objectives that require students to organise or generate content themselves. This may involve web publishing that includes not only text, but also audio and video content and images, enhancing the auditory or visual authenticity of the activities they undertake to meet the objectives.

You should also be particularly aware of the opportunities offered by web syndication and podcasting.

Web syndication

Those who use Web 2.0 applications in a global context (rather than a limited project-based context) value *web syndication*. This is where content in a website is made available to other websites to use, usually in the form of 'web feeds'. These web feeds are lists of new content from a website, for example, the latest post from a site. The web feed notifies subscribers of the latest content on your site and notifies you of the latest information on the sites of others. In this way a website (such as a blog) links to other websites with a common interest. By choosing the web feeds you want to use (subscribing) you can tailor the connections you make with others through your website, or have the latest information emailed directly to you through an *aggregator*.

There are several formats for web syndication. They are collectively called RSS feeds (for Really Simple Syndication or Rich Site Summary), and RDF (Resource Description Framework Site Summary), and they use a site's metadata to generate the feed.

Web feeds are useful from an academic perspective to keep track of new information in your area which can be relevant to you and your students.

Social bookmarking sites allow users to build content they can share using RSS feeds, while aggregators allow organisation of the content that is generated.

Podcasts

Podcasting is used to deliver audio or video to users as mp3 or mp4 files downloaded from the internet. The audio or video file itself is not a podcast, nor is an embedded file in a webpage.

Did you know ...?

It is the RSS technology which turns a media file into a podcast. The files are downloaded to a computer or portable mp3 player for use at the user's convenience. The files are stored (uploaded) on a specific server which facilitates their download. Web feeds are a feature of podcasting servers, as they are for blogs. They 'push' new mp3/4 files out to users. You may have accessed podcasts of radio programmes and used the 'feed' when you requested future programmes to be sent directly to your computer. You may use podcasts of relevant radio programmes as resources for your students. The availability of podcast material is rapidly expanding and this is changing the way media is broadcast.

The downside of podcasting, from the perspective of online learning design, is that there is a tendency to use it to replicate face-to-face teaching by podcasting lectures, without thinking about reconceptualising teaching to take advantage of what the technology offers. Barnes and Tynan (2007, p. 192) make this point in the following comment:

> Most podcasts are last year's lecture in digital format. Student remixing of podcasts, use of syndication to pool collective responses and other more active learning approaches are losing out to those that see podcasting as a high-tech alternative to the audio cassette of the 1980s. To avoid this outcome, university policy-makers and teaching staff alike need to listen to the call for fresh pedagogies ...

Mobile technologies and content

Specialist portable electronic devices for reading text, taking photos and recording audio are continually coming on the market. They range from laptop computers designed for annotating (e.g., Tablet PCs) and reading text (e.g., iBooks) to mp3 players (e.g., iPods) and mobile phones (e.g., iPhones). Apple Inc specialises in such idevices. They have many benefits, such as reducing the load of books that students carry and facilitating creation of content by both teachers and students. Building the use of such portable devices into learning activities for students raises an equity issue for those who cannot afford the device or a funding issue for the institution or faculty if the devices are provided for students.

Portable digital devices such as cameras and voice recorders enable you as a teacher and your students to easily create content in different forms. This allows you to add visual and aural dimensions to your teaching materials addressing a range of learning styles with images, video and audio. It similarly increases the ways in which students can present their responses to learning activities or assessment tasks.

Even newer options ...

Software which uses 'audit trail' data to determine 'characteristics' of users (learners) can help to tailor learning for an individual based on previous choices that they have made. In the commercial sector these Web 3.0 applications will enable advertisers to target advertisements to those who are most likely to 'buy', thereby not wasting marketing on those who go into 'mute' mode. As for Web 2.0 applications, Web 3.0 is more a case of using the data more effectively and efficiently, in this instance by adding new metadata to the web, rather than creating a new paradigm.

Another development to be aware of, which could affect your options, is the proliferation of open source applications (named because of the free availability of the source code for modification) which are challenging the rigid and costly proprietary learning management systems, potentially providing for greater customisation at institutional level. Nevertheless, as Dron (2007a, p. 219) explains:

> Open source is an approach, not a technology, so it requires programmers with relevant skills to implement changes. This makes it very far from free to implement successfully within an institutional context, and the cost may be similar to or greater than that of the commercial equivalents.

The open source collaboration tool Google Wave promises to facilitate online interaction and collaboration through seamless integration of internet capabilities.

* * *

While the summary of technology options in these sections does not cover all of the huge range of possibilities you could consider, you should now have some sense of the kind of online learning tools that you might use to allow students to meet the objectives you have specified. You will need to choose your options within the constraints of the technology options that are readily available to you, which we discussed earlier, and also bearing in mind the kinds of student support, management and administrative issues which we will address in the following sections.

You were probably aware, as we moved through some of the technology options, that you had a clearer idea of how you might implement some of them, compared to others. We will now look at some further issues relating to teaching with technology which you will need to think about before you make a final decision about your technology options. We will cover additional issues which relate to online learning design and development in Chapter 3, and to online assessment in Chapter 4.

Student support

We have already mentioned the benefits of institutional systems in relation to the backup procedures and access to technical support that are usually associated with them. The support issues that you need to consider when you are choosing your technology options include support for your students and support for you in managing the environment. It is likely that you will be responsible for much of the former, at least in terms of guiding students to the support that is available for them. In relation to the technologies you choose, you should be able to:

- develop contingency plans for unexpected technical problems, and communicate these to your students;

- ensure that appropriate support systems are in place for students and that they know how to access them, taking into consideration issues such as access and equity, variations in competence with the technology, the needs of international students and any costs or ethical issues; and

- ensure that students are able to access the sites or systems required (issues may include problems with usernames and passwords, browser configuration, or lack of broadband access if they are using dial-up modems from remote sites).

Remember that each additional tool you use in online teaching may involve a learning curve for your students so you may need to consider whether they have used these tools before in the context of their characteristics as learners which you addressed in Chapter 1. If any of the above are likely to be problematic, you may need to reconsider your options.

You will also need to think through how you will communicate important information to your students in order to support them. If you are not teaching in a context that includes face-to-face contact, you will need to consider carefully how you will provide instructions and perhaps give students the opportunity to practise. Two-way synchronous communication may be beneficial in this situation but it may not be possible to arrange unless you have face-to-face access to your students. Online chat, desktop videoconferencing or web conferencing potentially create additional barriers because they can be difficult in managing group communication.

> **For example ...**
>
> If you are thinking of running a synchronous chat session for students you will need to support them by having clear guidelines related to attendance, behaviour (netiquette), style and length of posts. It is wise to have a 'trial run' with colleagues if you are new to online chat.

Management and administrative issues

While having access to technology and to technical support are fundamental to successful teaching or assessment, you also need to know how to use the technology, and especially how to use it in pedagogically appropriate ways, in order to be able to communicate relevant teaching information to your students. Even though you are making your technology choices based on pedagogical decisions determined by the learning objectives, you may still need assistance to reconceptualise your teaching in order to teach effectively in this environment, drawing on the knowledge that has already been generated in the field.

The quickest way to do this is to check out the staff development opportunities that are easily available to you in relation to the technologies that you are considering. As well as formal staff development offerings, this might include talking to colleagues who have already used the technologies and gaining advice from them. We will consider some specific issues relating to pedagogy and online design and development in Chapter 3 but at this point it is important to establish whether or not this support exists.

An important general point to think about now is that if you have identified multiple objectives which suggest multiple technologies, it is probably best to scale back your plans and begin with the objectives that you consider to be most important and the technologies that will be simplest for you to manage. If you are teaching in a face-to-face or blended learning environment, consider dealing with only one component first, so that you can trial and evaluate that before adding others. If you are planning a fully online course, you will need to encompass all of the objectives but it is still best to start with technologies that you and your students are familiar with, if possible.

You also need to think about the nature of the technologies themselves, and their implications in terms of management and administration, including the workload for both you and your students.

For example ...

Online quizzes often involve a high start-up workload for you which may involve creating and assembling a database of questions that can be randomised, and including feedback on each correct and incorrect response. But once this job is done the task is automated.

In contrast, online discussions or wiki projects may involve little initial effort (though you may have administrative tasks involved in sorting students into groups), but then you need to organise moderation of the discussion. Keeping track of large numbers of messages can be complex for you and your students and involve a considerable workload. If you are assessing online discussion, you will have the further tasks involved with identifying assessment criteria and then analysing contributions to determine the extent to which criteria are met.

Deciding your options

You should now be in a good position to decide what your options are in terms of your choice of technologies. Your decision will be embedded in the pedagogical decisions you made in Chapter 1 and will be particularly driven by your identification of learning objectives. You will have noticed how each of the factors you have considered in this chapter has narrowed your options and provided a clearer focus on the technologies you will need. In practice, depending on your knowledge of available technologies, this process may be almost instantaneous. What we have aimed to do in this chapter is to break down this process into some of its component parts and illustrate the importance of keeping your eye firmly fixed on the pedagogical factors underlying your choice.

While there are further important issues to be addressed in Chapter 3 in relation to online learning design and development, the issues you have covered so far should be sufficient to enable you to decide *what* you will need in terms of technologies. These subsequent decisions will determine *how* you will use the technologies you have chosen.

Illustrating the ideas in this chapter ...

To illustrate what we have covered in this chapter, we continue Suzy's story which began in Chapter 1.

Suzy's story continued ...

My plan for use of the online environment began with the idea of an assessment task where students, working in groups, would create digital responses reflecting a practical (but fictional) context for identifying and discussing key issues in relation to infant and toddler care and education programmes. In doing this they would be critically examining relevant literature and relating it to their own experience.

To allow students to meet these objectives I planned to use the university's learning management system to provide the space for students to publish and share their work, and respond to the work of other groups in the online discussion forum. I believe strongly in working with the technologies that the university offers as this ensures technical support. I think that there is a danger of getting seduced by the technology if you work outside the university's systems. This carries a related danger of focusing on the technology (and the issues it raises) at the expense of the pedagogy.

I was aware, however, that in creating their digital responses (which could be in any form the students chose), they might need to develop new skills. In this sense, I planned to position the students' technology selection as a means of solving a problem (how to present their response). I was keen to push the boundaries with them in this way, and encourage innovation. I wanted students to solve these technical problems together, teaching each other and using tutorial time for this, if necessary.

> I did not envisage any other major student support, management or administrative issues related to the selection or implementation of technologies because I was using the university's systems and would be able to support the students in the face-to-face environment.

Summary

Drawing on the learning objectives you identified in Chapter 1, this chapter has covered some of the main issues that you need to consider in identifying your technology options. You have now thought about the affordances of the technologies you require, as determined by these objectives, and the role of your institution's policies and infrastructure in influencing your options. You have looked at a range of technologies that are available for use in education and you have considered some student support, management and administrative issues that you may need to address to finalise your choice.

You should now be clear about what your technology options are, taking into consideration any additional factors relating to your learning and teaching context that you did not think about in Chapter 1. In Chapter 3 we will move on to the design and development decisions you now need to make, which will bring you back to thinking about the nature of student learning.

Following is a continuation of the checklist which you began in Chapter 1. It encompasses the main planning stages we have covered in this chapter. If you are able to answer 'Yes' to most questions here, you will be ready to begin the design of your online environment. If your answer to most questions is 'No' (and assuming that your initial plans from Chapter 1 are in place) you will probably need to undertake further exploration of possible learning technologies. Remember that using technologies supported by your institution will probably be the easiest way to start, even if it involves some modifications to your plans (which do not threaten the learning or assessment benefits). If you need to explore the technologies further, developing the skills to use them is one dimension, but exploring how to use them effectively for learning or assessment is most important.

Are you able to identify ...	Yes	Unsure	No
9. Some technologies which offer the affordances that will allow students to meet online the learning objectives you have identified?			
10. How your institution's policies and infrastructure will affect the technologies you choose?			
11. The specific technologies that you will select for online learning or assessment?			
12. The support that your students might need in order to use these technologies, and how this support will be provided?			
13. The management and administrative issues that you need to deal with as you begin to teach or assess using these technologies, and strategies for dealing with them?			
14. Any other factors that you may need to consider in deciding your technology options? (Specify below.)			

Note

1. In this book we use the terms 'learning management system' or 'LMS' to refer to proprietary learning management systems and virtual learning environments.

3

Online learning design and development

Introduction

The learning objectives which you identified in Chapter 1, and which guided your selection of technologies in Chapter 2, should continue to drive the planning of your online learning design, which we cover in this chapter. They will also guide the design of online assessment, which we will begin to consider in this chapter but address in more detail in Chapter 4.

In Chapter 1, when we asked you to think about how students learn, we referred to two learning theories that have been important in higher education (phenomenography and constructivism) and noted that constructivism has been particularly influential in the field of educational technology. We will begin this chapter with some further comments about theories and models which may be useful in guiding your online learning design. It is the process of designing your online environment which will clarify the need to reconceptualise your teaching which we introduced in Chapter 1.

Then, with your objectives in mind, we will address some important elements of online learning design. These include learning activities (both individual and collaborative, and the provision of feedback on them) as well as the resources and support you will provide for your students. We will refer to both pre-Web 2.0 and Web 2.0 applications in considering these aspects of design.

Following this we will ask you to think about some of the issues you may face in developing your online environment because, along with the issues you considered in Chapter 2, these may also impact on the options available to you. We will then summarise some of the general student support, management and administrative issues that may affect the implementation of your design. By the end of this chapter you should have a good grasp of how to design and implement your online learning environment, prior to considering some specific aspects of online assessment in Chapter 4.

You should keep in mind as you work through this chapter that you do not have to include 'everything' in your online environment the first time that you implement it. Online learning design is an *iterative* process and you will finetune your environment over time as you gain experience and feedback. It is best to start with small, manageable components if you can, rather than trying to do too much and alienating students if they have problems. Such problems experienced early in a teaching period can override the advantages to learning that you hoped your environment would offer.

Theories and models guiding online learning design

Online learning can be regarded as a continuum from *classroom-enhanced* online learning where the technology is used within the classroom or lecture theatre, through *blended learning* which involves 'the thoughtful integration of classroom face-to-face learning experiences with online learning experiences' (Garrison & Kanuka, 2004, p. 96) to *fully online learning*. Except for classroom-enhanced online learning, a fundamental difference between face-to-face teaching and teaching online is that there is some degree of separation between learners, and between teacher and learners. A useful way of thinking about this issue, as a first step in reconceptualising your teaching for online learning, is to draw on transactional distance theory (Moore, 2007), which comes from the field of distance education.

Transactional distance theory

The key idea of transactional distance theory is that when there is separation between teachers and learners, you have transactional distance which involves psychological (rather than geographical) distance. This distance is bridged through the appropriate balance of *structure* (course design) and *dialogue*, considered in the context of the expected level of *learner autonomy* and the nature of the particular programme.

Structure and dialogue are usually seen as having an inverse relationship: when structure is high and dialogue is low, you have high transactional distance; when structure is low and dialogue is high, you have low transactional distance. However, Moore (1993) noted that a combination of both high structure and high dialogue can reduce transactional distance. The expected level of learner autonomy will often help to determine the appropriate balance.

For example ...

- Postgraduate students generally have a high degree of autonomy as learners and may need less structure than a group primarily consisting of first year undergraduate students.

- A school leaver has come from a highly structured environment where others (teachers and parents) keep track of their progress and they are repeatedly reminded of expectations and deadlines. Students making the transition to higher education and working in online learning environments may need support through both structure and dialogue in managing their own learning.

We suggest combining high dialogue and high structure for *fully online* learning, irrespective of learning autonomy, for the following reasons:

> ... a classroom can support low dialogue and low structure (-D-S) in the online components used because the face-to-face context provides for low transactional distance. However, in contexts characterised by medium transactional distance (such as blended learning environments), an inverse relationship between structure and dialogue is evident, though the specific aspects of the relationship will depend on the context and on the autonomy of the learners. As transactional distance becomes potentially greater in off-campus and transnational units which are wholly or partly online, there appear to be benefits in both high dialogue and high structure (+D+S) to meet learners' needs. (Benson & Samarawickrema, 2009, pp. 10–11)

Moore (2004) places his ideas within a constructivist framework, but whether or not you are drawing on constructivist ideas to guide your online learning design, it may be helpful for you to keep dialogue, structure and learner autonomy in mind as you consider the design of specific components of your online environment.

Some online learning models

In addition to theoretical perspectives for conceptualising online learning, a number of specific models have been proposed for guiding design. Whereas theories help to explain how learning occurs, models provide frameworks for implementing these ideas. We will briefly mention four models here. Depending on your objectives, you may find one (or more) of them helps you to conceptualise your online environment. All of them focus on the importance of activity by the learner.

1. Oliver and Herrington (2001) see the online environment as consisting of three major components: *activities*, *resources* and *supports*. Using a constructivist perspective, they recommend beginning with the design of student learning activities. These will be determined by the learning objectives and should involve authentic ('real world') tasks. Then design the resources and supports that students will need to complete the activities. Activities, resources and supports are all integrated in the design of assessment. Oliver and Herrington suggest that the most successful forms of assessment occur when the learning tasks and assessment tasks merge, taking the view that clever design of assessment tasks can provide strong supports for learning.

2. Salmon's (2003) five-step model for teaching and learning online is useful for conceptualising teaching if you are planning to use online discussion groups. This is based on social constructivism. Salmon suggests that teaching and learning using online discussion involves five stages: (1) access and motivation; (2) online socialisation; (3) information exchange; (4) knowledge construction; and (5) development (where participants become responsible for their own learning). The model describes the types of roles you need to play at each stage to get your online discussion activities working effectively.

3. Garrison and Anderson (2003) draw on the collaborative potential of online discussion for creating a learning community to present a community of inquiry model of online teaching and learning. They suggest that within a community of inquiry an educational experience has three primary components: cognitive presence, social presence and teacher presence, and that this framework has potential for

structuring, guiding and assessing online learning approaches, strategies and techniques.

4. Laurillard (2002) uses a phenomenographic perspective to suggest that learning is based on the interaction of four characteristics: teacher's conceptual knowledge, student's conceptual knowledge, teacher's constructed world and student's experiential world. Using a conversational framework, the learning process is seen as a dialogue between teacher and students, involving *discursive, adaptive, interactive* and *reflective* components. She uses these characteristics as criteria for judging how learning and teaching systems which use educational technology are best used.

For the purposes of this chapter, it is important to recognise that there are a number of existing models, including those above, which you could explore or adapt to guide your online teaching or assessment. You will find that use of any of these models to guide the planning of your online environment will involve quite a different approach compared to teaching face-to-face. When teaching involves the collaborative activities of groups of learners using Web 2.0 applications, the implications for teaching are even greater and the idea of transactional control, which we outline below, provides a way to conceptualise some of the issues.

Transactional control

For students to take advantage of Web 2.0 applications for learning, you need to consider who will be in control in that environment, the learners or the teacher. Bottom-up control by the group is usually necessary to gain the benefits of group collaboration but you might need to provide considerable support (through dialogue and structure) *outside* the Web 2.0 environment to nurture the group process, but avoid interfering within it. Dron (2007a) uses the concept of transactional control, which is related to transactional distance theory, to examine the control issues which emerge in the use of social software, suggesting that transactional control is concerned with choices, either by teacher or learners. He notes the potential for learners to generate dialogue through structure and structure through dialogue. Dron explains that transactional control theory 'does not aim to replace transactional distance theory as it says nothing significant of the psychological gap between learner and teacher, but it helps to explain some of its dynamics', commenting that '[s]tructure equates to teacher control, dialogue to negotiated control, and autonomy to learner control' (Dron, 2007b, p. 60).

> **For example ...**
>
> If you want your students to undertake a group project in a wiki, you may want them to exercise their autonomy through *learner control* in this environment. However, you may also recognise that they will need considerable guidance. To do this, you might embed the link to the wiki in a site within your LMS and provide detailed instructions on this site, exercising your *teacher control*. You might also have a related discussion space on this site for dialogue with your students to answer any queries that they might have (*negotiated control*). While you and the students could interact in this space, the discussion *within* the wiki would be for the students' own use, allowing them to communicate as they prepare their project.

We will now return to your learning objectives which will lead us into addressing some of the key pedagogical components you will need to consider as part of your online learning design. As we do this, we will be referring to the concepts mentioned in this section again so that you can see how they might be helpful in informing your design.

Aligning learning objectives, activities and assessment

A useful design principle that comes from the field of higher education and is informed by constructivist learning theory is that of *constructive alignment* (Biggs & Tang, 2007). This is the concept that when you design learning, you need to make sure that the objectives, activities and assessments are aligned. This will occur if you design learning activities that will allow students to meet the objectives, and assessment tasks that examine whether the objectives have been met. Although there have been some criticisms of this principle, often because it places definition (and control) of the learning objectives firmly in the hands of the teacher rather than the learner, it is nevertheless a useful concept for guiding online learning design. If your subject requires that students design their own learning objectives, then *your* objectives can specify this, and they could also specify that students will need to design and align appropriate tasks to allow them to meet these objectives if this is their responsibility.

For example ...

- For an *objective* which requires students to critically discuss a controversial topic (e.g., the use of Wikipedia in research), students could engage in an online debate (the *activity*) and then write a summary of arguments and synthesise a 'best reasoned' outcome (the *assessment*).

- If the *objective* required students to prepare a learning contract for work that they would undertake on a fieldwork placement, then the initial *activity* might be that they negotiate, identify, determine or simply write their own objectives. In this case the *assessment* of the learning contract would include the appropriateness of the learning objectives and the extent to which the students have met them.

In each of these examples the activity helps students achieve the objective and the assessment provides evidence of the extent to which they are successful. Keep in mind that the activities you design and/or the assessment may help students to achieve more than one learning objective.

For example ...

The activity of debating which is designed to allow students to demonstrate their ability to critically discuss a controversial topic may also address related learning objectives which require students to demonstrate communication skills, or argumentation skills.

Students will engage more readily when they can see that activities and assessment tasks can help them to achieve multiple learning objectives.

The principle of constructive alignment also sits well with the suggestion by Oliver and Herrington (2001) that successful forms of assessment occur when the learning tasks and assessment tasks merge, providing motivation for students to complete the activities. This means that there will be some overlap between the concepts covered in this chapter and in Chapter 4.

Designing online learning activities, resources and support

If you support the idea of active learning, then the design of the learning activities will be at the heart of your online learning design, providing the means for students to meet the learning objectives, as outlined above. As we mentioned earlier, Oliver and Herrington (2001) see the online environment as consisting of three major components: *activities*, *resources* and *supports*, and they suggest that you begin with the design of your learning activities. This is a simple and intuitive model which we will use to consider these three elements of online learning design.

Activities can take a variety of forms, depending on the nature of the related learning objective, and on the technologies available to you which you considered in Chapter 2. These include interactions of students with each other, with the teacher, with content and with the computer interface through tasks that provide an automated response. In this chapter we will focus particularly on tasks that involve interaction between users, and on those that involve interaction with or creation of content. We will begin in the following section by using asynchronous online discussion to highlight some of the opportunities that communication activities provide and some of the design issues that you need to consider. Activities with automated responses will be addressed in Chapter 4 since these are frequently used in the context of assessment. We include some specific suggestions relating to resources and supports as we consider the learning activities. This will help us apply the model and attend to these three elements of the online learning environment.

This approach should help you to clarify how you might reconceptualise your teaching for online learning because it suggests that the 'content' you may have previously presented in your lectures now becomes part of the *resources* you provide for students to assist them to complete the activities. The affordances of the technologies you have selected will have implications for the design of both activities and resources.

Oliver and Herrington (2001, p. 55) refer to learning supports as 'the processes and procedures by which learners are assisted in their learning activities, by which feedback and guidance is provided to them and by which their involvement in the learning setting is encouraged and strengthened'. If you draw on transactional distance theory as mentioned earlier, then you could think about the appropriate balance of dialogue and structure (in the context of the expected level of learner autonomy) to help inform the design of the *support* that you will include.

Interaction between users: online discussion activities

Online communication can be used for a diversity of purposes, ranging from simple socialisation to facilitating high level cognitive and collaborative participation in the completion of learning tasks which are central to assessment. You can craft questions for online discussion relating to learning objectives within each category in Bloom's taxonomy (The Pennsylvania State University, 2007). This is illustrated in Table 3.1.

Table 3.1 Online discussion questions for different cognitive processes based on Bloom's (revised) taxonomy

Cognitive process dimension	Examples of activities	Examples of question types
1. Remember	Recall previously learnt knowledge e.g., Answer a factual question.	Who; What; Where; When; Why; How; Label; State; Recall; etc.
2. Understand	Demonstrate understanding of the meaning of subject material e.g., Explain to a colleague.	Give an example; State in your own words; Demonstrate; Explain; Translate; Classify; Summarise; etc.
3. Apply	Apply subject material to a new situation e.g., Work through a case study.	Predict; Choose the best alternative; Judge the effects of; etc.
4. Analyse	Analyse components or relationships e.g., Review journal articles.	Distinguish; Identify; What assumptions are made?; What motives?; What inconsistencies are present?; What is the main idea or theme?; etc.
5. Evaluate	Demonstrate ability to judge and defend particular issues	Appraise; Judge; Criticise; Defend; Which is more important/moral/accurate/logical/valid?; etc.
6. Create	Demonstrate ability to develop a new approach in a specific situation e.g., Develop a new creative piece of work.	Create; Develop; Propose an alternative; How would you test?; Plan?; Design?; How else would you do this?; etc.

If you were using Laurillard's (2002) conversational framework, designing your discussion groups would provide very clear guidelines for your interactions with students.

For example ...

The *discursive* environment enables conversation as a form of *interactivity* between teacher and learners to facilitate learning through the exchange of views about a topic. Asynchronous communication increases opportunities for *reflection* about one's views. Modifying ideas as a result of discussion is a process of *adaptation*. The capacity for iterative dialogue allows for the conceptual change involved in learning.

Several benefits of online discussion are summarised in Table 3.2. Some of these aspects may help you respond to the characteristics of your students, and the contexts of learning and teaching, that you considered in Chapter 1.

Whatever your use of online discussion, students will need guidance on its purpose and how to use it. If you are teaching in a blended environment much of the support you give to students can occur face-to-face. Students can be 'walked through' the online environment and expectations can be discussed. When you expect students to engage in discussion online only, you will need to build considerable support into the online environment and orient them to it.

Orienting your students

Once you have planned how you will use your discussion groups, one of the first things you need to think about is how you will communicate this information to your students and provide an opportunity to answer their questions. An *orientation* session or some prepared orientation information is a very important aspect of the support you need to provide to help students to understand what is being asked of them and why.

| Table 3.2 | Some benefits of online discussion |

Aspect	Advantages
Students can think, plan and/or reflect before they write.	This may be a particular advantage for students for whom English is a second language, or students who are shy or lacking in confidence.
Students express themselves in written form, rather than orally.	This might suit the learning styles of some students, allowing them to participate more easily.
Responses to questions are available for all to see.	This minimises the number of similar questions asked of the teacher, and maximises the number of students with access to the response.
Off-campus students are supported.	Discussion groups provide feedback on progress, and allow social interaction between the students themselves and with their teachers.
Time zone differences are accommodated.	Discussion groups allow interactions between students and teachers when time zone differences prevent easy synchronous communication.
Time scheduling differences are accommodated.	Online discussions enable students to communicate at times which suit them.

For example ...

If you are using the discussion tool in an LMS you could include an introduction to students in an html page or a discussion post with an explanation of the purpose of different discussion topics. This orientation may need to include broad issues relating to the use of the online technologies, as well as the specific way you will be using them. If your students are new to online learning, you may need to include simple instructions on how to navigate your site and how to view and post discussion messages. And don't forget to tell them about how to obtain technical or other assistance.

It is easy to neglect this important stage and feel pressure to start the 'real' work. However, you will usually be rewarded many times over if you handle orientation well, as you will reduce student problems which have an impact on your own time. As we noted earlier, Salmon (2003) suggests that access and motivation followed by online socialisation are the first two steps in teaching using online discussion groups and you should make sure that you allow sufficient time for students to complete these steps.

Access and socialisation

Technical problems related to students accessing online discussions are less frequent now that learning management systems are well established. Nevertheless, you may need to consider issues such as the following.

- What computer and network access do your students have?
- Do they have access to adequate IT support?
- What are your students' IT skills? You may need to consider whether they have used these tools before – for example, a first year or a mature age student may not have encountered the technology.

Once you have addressed the technical issues, students may still need some time to become comfortable with your expectations. This will happen more easily if you allow for it as part of the orientation stage. The first step in establishing an online discussion may be achieved with messages of introduction, or about other social matters, or icebreaking activities. This can help foster a sense of community, particularly in classes where students may not meet face-to-face. This step may overlap with discussion topics specifically designed for support. You could ask students to introduce themselves in their first message. You would set the expectation by introducing yourself (thereby providing a model for them). This could be conducted as a separate social discussion topic or be part of a topic associated with a particular activity, depending on the characteristics of the learners, and the nature of the activity. The following example is a suggestion for a first message to introduce students to your expectations.

For example ...

Welcome to the online discussion area of the subject XYX1234. This subject has several different discussion topics – one for each module of the subject, as well as this Introductions topic. One of the 'housekeeping' requirements of online discussions is making sure that you post your messages into the correct topic. Please ensure that you open the relevant topic before you create your message. Use a descriptive term for your message subject, so that others can easily identify what your message is about. If you wish to respond to someone else's message, make sure you open their message first, and then click the Reply button. This will mean that all messages will display correctly as 'threaded discussions'.

Try to keep your messages to only a few paragraphs – none of us want to read huge tracts online! If you have a large amount of information to share, you can attach a Word document to your discussion message.

Feel free to use this Introduction's topic for any social messages – this is a great opportunity to get to know each other and build networks which may be useful in your professional careers!

I hope that you enjoy the unit and find it stimulating and informative ☺.

You could then ask the students to complete an icebreaking activity or you could include this as part of the posting in which they introduce themselves.

For example ...

■ Post a paragraph about yourself, stating where you come from and why you chose to study this unit. Read the posts of others.

■ Search the internet for a line from a movie or a song which captures something about the place where you come from (anything except ... Frankly my dear ... and you know the rest). Include the quote, the name of the movie or song, the year it was released, the director/actor or author and why you chose it.

■ For local students: Estimate how far from the campus you live, post your name, location and the distance from the campus on the list of students in the discussion, in order from closest to

> furthest from the campus. For example, I will post first. I live in Fairfield which is 20 kilometres from the campus so I will write 'my name, Fairfield, 20 km from campus'. If you post second and live in Chadstone which is five kilometres from the campus, insert your name and details before mine. You can do this by replying to my post adding your details to your message and copying mine below. When each person has copied the list and inserted their details we will have a list of class participants and locations.
>
> ■ For off-campus or transnational students: Look around you. If you are indoors and near a window, look outside. Now describe your surroundings. Try to convey some distinctive characteristics of your place of study and your city, region or country (including the weather!).

Such icebreaking activities may seem trivial but they give you and your students an opportunity to get to know each other and identify as a group, making support easier. They also give students useful connections for supporting themselves such as arranging shared transport (if students live close to each other) or setting up social or study groups (which are often particularly valued by students who are studying off-campus or transnationally).

Online discussion in individual activities

Once you have completed the access and socialisation steps, you can focus on the activities that will help students to meet your specified objectives. Salmon (2002) uses the term 'e-tivities' for these learning activities. She considers that each 'e-tivity' should have the following key features:

■ an illustrative title;

■ a small piece of information, stimulus or challenge to initiate it (which Salmon calls the 'spark');

■ online action which includes individual participants posting a response (the 'invitation');

■ an interactive or participative element – such as responding to the postings of others (the 'action and interaction');

- elapsed time allowed and requirements for posting times specified; and
- summary, feedback or critique from an e-moderator.

Salmon provides examples of 'e-tivities' appropriate for each of the stages of her five stage model (Salmon, 2002). At Stage 3 (information exchange) you would be expecting interaction between students which requires comment on the contributions of others.

For example ...

Stage 3 learning activities might include:

- answering questions posed by you;
- interviewing members of the community and reporting back to the class; or
- researching a given topic and sharing the results.

However, it is important to set specific boundaries around what you expect students to do. Activities which have too many components may result in students tending to write 'essays' online instead of discussion contributions. Encourage students to keep contributions simple, focused and limited in length (no more than one screen of text).

For example ...

Provide instructions for students such as the following.

Each week, I will post the weekly problem into this discussion area. Choose an aspect of the problem to study, research the problem and write a commentary summarising the key points. Post your responses in the same discussion area as a 'reply'. Please keep your messages to a manageable one or two paragraphs. Feel free to reply to each other – either to confirm or question your colleagues' responses. I will summarise your results and provide feedback on your collective efforts at the end of each Friday.

Make sure that your questions or topics do, in fact, lend themselves to discussion. Closed response questions (requiring a 'Yes' or No' answer) do not generate discussion unless you also ask for the reasons for the response. Once one person has posted a response, consider what motivation there is for other students to post. Similarly, avoid questions with factual answers as they leave no room for multiple contributions once one person has answered the question correctly.

For example ...

- Comment on the views about climate change expressed in the article, explaining whether you agree or disagree, and giving a reason for your opinion. If someone has already expressed your point of view, provide another reason, or add further information to support the reasons that have already been presented.

  rather than

  Do you agree with the views about climate change expressed in the article?

- A medical student explained the structure of bone, at the cellular level, to a patient in the following way. [Insert explanation here.] Make one comment about the appropriateness of this explanation (you could refer either to the factual information or the way it is explained). Make sure that your comment has not already been made by someone else.

  rather than

  How would you explain the structure of bone to a patient, at the cellular level?

Online discussion in group activities

If you are using online discussion specifically to support the idea of students' learning through collaboration in groups, the concept of a *community of inquiry* may be helpful in guiding your design. In this context a community of learners forms 'an essential, core element of an educational experience where higher-order learning is the desired outcome' (Garrison & Anderson, 2003, p. 22). The success of an online community for learning relies on careful design of activities and supports which give meaning to a collaborative pursuit so students are learning from and with each other rather than alongside each other.

The use of online discussion groups for collaboration can take a number of different forms. The following examples illustrate forms that involve authentic learning tasks. However, note that these are complex activities that require careful planning and organisation. Students need to know exactly what is required of them, and when, which means that you will need to provide a high level of support.

Examples include ...

Debating: Introduce a contentious or current issue, and ask groups of students to argue each side of the debate.

Case study: Provide a 'real' problem for students to work on and present a submission to the client. For example:

- Provide a genetic analysis of a small breeding population for a zoo.
- Prepare architectural plans for a public building to meet certain specifications.
- Conduct a survey in the community and prepare a marketing strategy for a proposed product.

Role playing activities: Assign students to different roles in a specific situation, and require them to complete certain activities. For example:

- Form a law firm, and act for a client against a competing law firm.
- Play different roles in a social work/counselling situation.
- Take on different roles in a school setting, and produce reports for the school board, including different points of view from the different roles undertaken.

If students are to collaborate effectively on group projects online they need the same teamwork skills as they would need in face-to-face collaboration. These skills of negotiation, decision making, task and time management need time and support to develop. Students are often initially reluctant to collaborate with their peers to produce a shared outcome. They may feel that others are benefiting from their efforts or that a group submission is not of the high standard that they would achieve alone. You may need to provide students with specific support mechanisms for collaborating, and develop a marking scheme which assesses and rewards individual contributions (more about this in Chapter 4). You could include successful teamwork as one of the learning objectives for your students.

When asking students to collaborate online you may have to articulate roles and responsibilities and give them some hints about how to deal with problems that arise. An awareness of the characteristics of your students and your own experience of them should help you to anticipate the difficulties they might have and enable you to prepare them adequately. When in doubt, ask them for their feelings about and experience of collaborating online. In designing the group activity think about how you will allocate students to groups: will you assign them or allow them to self-select (maybe via a sign-up sheet)? Students in friendship groups may use the discussion space you set up for the task for social communication. This may not matter if the online discussion is only used for convenience and flexibility, but if the process of collaboration is also important then a record of it will be required.

You might include in your design for student group work an expectation that students will take the moderating role. If you organise this, it is important that you provide them with guidance about how to undertake it.

For example ...

When students are working as a group, the group leader may take the role of discussion moderator. In such a case you would need to identify and assign roles to particular students, or let them know they should self assign these roles.

The success or otherwise of the activity is likely to be contingent on the level and organisation of the support that you provide.

For example ...

Below are some instructions for students who were asked to undertake the e-moderation role. They are based on general e-moderation guidelines from Salmon (2003). Note that these guidelines apply equally to online discussions which are not about group work and where students discuss any aspect of their work and receive feedback from peers.

1. Post your discussion question in your first message and invite responses. To get the discussion started it may be helpful to add (very briefly) two or three issues which you think need to be considered in answering the question.
2. Check the messages daily (at least).
3. Be ready to respond to contributions, and lead the discussion, but do not intervene too much: not more than one in four messages from you.
4. Be patient and always polite.
5. Be inclusive of and value all participants. Encourage non-participants to join in.
6. Find the unifying threads in a discussion: build, weave and summarise ideas constantly, keeping the focus on the main question but integrating related questions where appropriate.
7. Ideally, mention the names of contributors when summarising but be sure not to leave anyone out.
8. Do not let the discussion stray: if it is moving away from the question, bring it (politely) back on track.
9. At the end of the activity, summarise the main responses to the question which have emerged from the discussion and thank all participants.

Supporting online discussion activities

We have mentioned some specific aspects of support in relation to online discussion as we have moved through this section. Moderation of discussion can provide both general and specific support for students. The design of the forum sets up the online environment as a safe place for students where their concerns will be heard, by other students and/or by teaching staff. In this context it is important that you describe to students the level of support you are offering (for instance, when you will be in the online discussion space) and then adhere to this. Off-campus students often find that the availability of other students as part of a learning community is support in itself.

To complete this section, Table 3.3 summarises some common issues encountered in using online discussions with tips on dealing with them.

Table 3.3 Support issues and tips for online discussion

Issues	Tips
Students may be reluctant to demonstrate the limitations of their learning for all to see.	Provide a safe and supportive environment, encouraging all to participate.
If the discussion list is used as a record for assessment, then students may be unwilling to take risks in entering into discussion.	Develop appropriate assessment strategies, and stress the importance of participation to your students. Emphasise the relevant assessment criteria.
Some students are more comfortable in passive participation (or 'lurking') in discussion lists, just as they are in listening in face-to-face tutorials, rather than actively engaging in discussion.	Does this matter? If not, don't worry! If it does, design appropriate strategies to encourage participation.
Students may feel frustrated and negative about participating in online discussions if their comments go unanswered.	Tell your students when you will be online, and encourage fellow students to respond during other times. Make sure that all contributions are acknowledged.
Without body language cues, online communication can be misinterpreted.	Act as a role model for your students, e.g., post clear and simple messages, free of jargon or in-jokes.

Interaction between users: activities using other communication forms

Online chat

You are more likely to use online chat for supporting students undertaking a learning activity, rather than for implementing the activity itself, because of the difficulties in managing these synchronous sessions which we mentioned in Chapter 2. Difficulties include the time constraints of requiring everyone to be present at the same time, and difficulties in pacing text-based responses with replies to one message overlapping new messages and responses to previous messages. However, the sense of immediacy can itself be supportive for some students, giving them a feeling of being 'heard'.

Online videoconferencing and web conferencing

Videoconferencing is now common for conducting meetings enabling individuals to contribute from remote locations. If you are familiar with this type of meeting you will know that they require greater concentration than a face-to-face meeting. An online videoconference meeting has an additional challenge because the quality of the audio and video is limited by the bandwidth. For an activity where a small number of students collaborate with a clear purpose, online videoconferencing could be motivational.

For example ...

A small group of students studying interdisciplinary issues in health professional education could role play a meeting where each person represented a different discipline in discussing a case. Similarly, the technology could be used for one-to-one interactions where one student interviews or counsels a 'client'.

Managing web conferencing is often easier when one person is presenting to the group. The screen-based presentation lends itself to situations where the presenter has something to demonstrate, but interaction can be increased through activities such as polling and responding to questions from the 'audience'.

Mobile technologies

Mobile technologies may be an advantage in activities which require flexibility regarding time and place, though the ubiquitous presence of mobile phones means that you may consider uses for them even when there is no separation between you and students in time and place. They allow for immediate, personalised contact which can be either synchronous or asynchronous (as in text messaging) and used for either individual or group communication. If you expect your students to use their own mobile devices (telephones) for class-related activities, you should check first that they are willing to do this. If you then want to build this contact into your teaching, you can use this mode of communication for either providing information to them (such as, assignment advice or results), communicating with each other, or receiving messages from them.

For example ...

- Ask students on a field trip to text other members of their group (or the class) when they find a specimen.
- In a lecture, ask students to send questions as text messages. This allows them to interact with you without interrupting you: you can choose the time/s in the lecture that you will respond to the questions.

Jones, Edwards and Reid (2009) describe the use of mobile SMS messaging for first year undergraduate students where messaging supported face-to-face teaching and the implementation of student activities on the LMS site. Used in this way, mobile communication can have both a pedagogical and support function. There are other advantages of mobile devices in relation to interaction with and creation of content which we will consider in the following sections.

Tablet computer technologies are useful for engaging students in communicating with the teacher in class. The teacher is then able to share selected contributions with the class as a whole.

For example ...

You can ask students to contribute a response to a question which they share with the class via submission to you. This enables students in a large class to be actively involved in a constructivist approach to learning in a lecture environment.

Students could work in groups to submit a group response to an activity in class.

Tablet computers have particular benefits in conveying visual information that is difficult to produce quickly via a keyboard and requires specialised software.

> **For example ...**
>
> The ability to use 'digital ink' to produce, share, annotate and display hand-drawn diagrams and symbols is useful in disciplines such as mathematics, engineering or architecture, or in teaching languages such as Chinese or Japanese where characters are used for written communication.

Games, simulations and virtual worlds

Games, simulations and virtual worlds offer the promise of activities with rich interaction between users. We have mentioned previously that these environments are an unlikely choice if you are new to online teaching because of their complexity. However, simulated experiences which involve interaction between users (such as role plays) are not complex in terms of the software required (online discussion groups are sufficient), though they can still be complex in terms of design and implementation.

Interaction with content

The online environment, with its abundance of information, offers an excellent opportunity for students to develop research skills. Designing activities which foster students' abilities to search for, analyse, interpret, critique and summarise information helps them to develop important graduate attributes.

> **For example ...**
>
> ■ Ask students to find information online on a topic, summarise it and submit for viewing by other students. You could then ask them to critique information retrieved and summarised by another student.

> - Ask students working in groups each to find some information relevant to a particular topic and then work together to compile it.

Nearly every activity that you design will require students to interact with content in some way, for learning objectives relating to all cognitive processes in Bloom's (revised) taxonomy. As we mentioned earlier, this requires you to think about the resources that you will provide and it will often involve reconceptualising the material that you previously provided in lectures as part of these resources.

Design decisions include:

- How much 'content' will you provide, through material you develop yourself, readings that you identify and links to other resources? Will you give students all the resources they need or do you want them to develop research skills and find material themselves?

- What form will the resources take? For material that you develop yourself, your options include text, images, audio or video but how you design these components will be determined by the content and context. Be aware of potential problems with downloading and keep audio and video clips short (usually less than five minutes). If you are designing an authentic learning experience such as a case study or role play, the experience will determine the various (authentic) forms that the resources might take.

For example ...

- If the case study is a medical one, scans of actual medical records (in pdf format) will help students immerse themselves in the case study.

- If you are trying to describe the noise level in a factory, an audio file would be useful.

- In discussing a famous speech, a video excerpt from the speech may carry more information than a transcript. Remember the image of Martin Luther King and 'I have a dream... .'

How will you provide the resources? Again, for resources that you develop to be used as part of an authentic learning experience, the way you provide them, and the timing of this provision, will be determined by the learning experience.

For example ...

In analysing a case study you may give students the first part of the case with some guidelines for analysis, including questions about decisions they would make. You would then give them the next part of the case study and ask them to develop their analysis further. In this way the case unfolds as students work their way through 'episodes' of the story. This can help students work through the process of analysis rather than skipping to the end.

- What guidance will you need to provide for students to interact with content in the ways you require? How will you provide this guidance? This is an important support issue. Remember that tasks as simple as finding information take time and skill and students may need support to do that.

The wealth of information online makes it tempting to offer resources as web addresses (URLs). Students can easily become overwhelmed with more information than they can manage if you are giving them *all the good sites* you have found. For each resource that you consider, ask the question 'Do the students really need this in order to complete the activity successfully?' If the answer is 'No' but you think the resource is valuable for them you can tag some resources as 'additional' or 'advanced' and indicate that they are not essential. Annotating resources is also helpful so that students are aware of the content and value of each one. Categorising the resources is essential so that students understand what they are accessing and why. Remember that some resources take time to retrieve and students will lose confidence in them if they find that they are not useful.

When linking online resources to your subject site, consider the copyright implications. It is good practice to explain where the resource comes from.

For example ...

In using a resource from the Monash University Library you would enter the following in your list:

To support your first activity go to the short online tutorial on 'Citing and referencing' from the Monash University Library at *http://www.lib.monash.edu.au/tutorials/citing/*

Alternatively, you can enter a link to the university homepage and direct students to the relevant page. This can be confusing for students who get lost following directions through multiple links within a site.

Remember also that reusable learning objects created by multimedia developers which you can add to your LMS site may be available to provide simulated experiences for your students.

For example ...

In a nursing subject an interactive online exercise that replicates actual equipment operation can be used to teach student nurses how to operate particular types of equipment with safety. A multimedia version of a volumetric infusion pump allows students to work through the steps in using it, and gain a sense of what the equipment looks, sounds and feels like to use.

While complex and costly to develop yourself, it may be worthwhile searching to determine whether an appropriate piece of software that might meet your needs is already in existence either within your institution or externally.[1]

Mobile devices are also increasingly providing opportunities for interaction with content, through their ability to receive information, including visual material captured by others, and their web-browsing capabilities. Their ubiquity extends to places, such as locations in remote areas, where access to the internet may not be available. As always, the students' characteristics, the learning and teaching context and the learning objectives will determine the best ways of ensuring that students have the opportunities for interacting with content that they need.

Creation of content: individual and group activities

Students undertaking activities that involve creation of content will usually be working at the top level of the cognitive process dimension in Bloom's taxonomy. You will need to determine the degree of support they will need based on their previous academic experience. Because one of the key affordances of Web 2.0 applications is the ease with which users can create content online, this makes them a good choice for the design of activities where students collaborate in groups to create content.

For example ...

Earlier we gave the following illustration of a role play activity that students could undertake in an online discussion group.

Take on different roles in a school setting, and produce reports for the school board, including different points of view from the different roles undertaken.

If this task was undertaken in a wiki, students could develop, refine and produce the reports in the wiki's collaborative space. There would be no need to send around discussion postings with attachments to members of the group as the reports were developed. Students could use the associated discussion space within the wiki to plan their work and discuss issues relating to the developing documents.

Suzy's story provides another (non Web 2.0) example of how the online learning environment can support students' learning through the creation of content.

In this section we will briefly consider the following specific ways that the online learning environment can support creation of content, and some of the design issues involved, through the use of:

- e-portfolios
- blogs
- wikis
- shared documents
- student podcasting, and
- mobile technologies.

Note that the creation of content online, combined with the ready access to existing information online, means that plagiarism can occur very easily. Depending on the academic experience of your students, and the way that you want them to create content, you may need to provide specific advice about plagiarism and how to avoid it. They may need help to distinguish between the use of material or ideas without appropriate acknowledgement and mashups, where co-authored work legitimately combines original content with reuse of internet content from other sources.

E-portfolios

A portfolio is a useful format for collecting evidence of achievements and can form an important basis for preparation for the professions. The portfolio can become a rich assessment item, as well as assisting students to track their own learning. The inclusion of critical reflection extends the portfolio to allow assessment of this valuable graduate attribute.

Mathur and Murray (2006, p. 250) summarise some of the advantages of e-portfolios as follows.

1. Electronic portfolios can be edited, updated, retrieved, and instantly made available to several people simultaneously.

2. Electronic portfolios are user friendly. Voice recordings, digital pictures, and videos by the student, teacher, peers, and other raters can personalize electronic portfolios.

3. Electronic portfolios are designed to accept instant feedback from teachers, peers, and area experts, and provide exceptional flexibility to the process of learning and assessment.

4. Electronic portfolios make it possible to cross-reference a student's work across content areas. Different parts of the curriculum can be connected and cross-referenced easily.

5. Since it is possible to store, cross-reference, and retrieve student portfolios easily, instructors and administrators can retrieve student

work from past semesters and years to display them as examples for future students.

6. Electronic portfolios vividly describe and assess the learning processes and products.

They successfully document learning across curriculum and grade levels.

There are a number of software programs designed for the set up and maintenance of portfolios. In the absence of software with support at an institutional level, blogs provide an excellent vehicle for portfolios. Requiring students to maintain a blog for the semester has potential to address several objectives relating to individual and group learning. We will address other uses of blogs below.

Activities related to e-portfolios need to be supported with training in how to use the technology as well as the usual objectives and guidance on how to achieve the desired outcomes. You will need to liaise with your institution's technical team to design appropriate initial training on the functionality of the software, but you will also need ongoing technical support as students develop their portfolio and use the technical skills required. While some students may grasp the technology rapidly, others will need further training to use tools beyond the basics as their portfolio develops.

Blogs

As the name implies, a blog (weblog) is an obvious choice for activities that involve journalling and personal reflection. The online environment offers the ability for students to share their work easily with you and/ or other students and/or people beyond the classroom, as required, and receive feedback from them. Mathur and Murray (2006, p. 251) summarise some advantages of e-journals.

1. E-journals help in understanding changing contexts of learning and modifying expectations of tasks as needed.

2. Peers, experts, and instructors alike may review the entries and respond to questions and problems. Since it is possible to receive frequent and immediate responses, electronic journal entries often foster relationship building.

3. E-journals are an important way of obtaining multiple perspectives to a problem and eliciting several solutions to a problem.

4. E-journaling is used to brainstorm and reflect on one's own work and that of others.

5. Online journaling provides a collaborative learning environment that encourages students to question and to resolve difficulties within a social context.

6. Sharing journal entries helps students see how others think and work.

Most school leavers will be familiar with blog technology but mature learners may need support in setting up a blog and understanding access issues. An advantage of blogs is that they are easy to set up and use so you will be able to provide most of the support students need in terms of using the technology.

For example ...

An introductory activity in which students set up a blog and make an initial entry may be sufficient to ensure they know how to use the technology.

Reflective practice may be intuitive for some students but others may be unfamiliar with it. You may need to explain what it means, why and how you expect students to engage with it as an activity, and the consequences of their doing so.

For example ...

In using a blog for reflective practice you may ask students to post a statement about their goals in the subject or the course (or start simply with their goals in the activity) and give the post an appropriate title or subject line. This will provide them with technical practice at making a post to their blog and start the process of structuring the blog for the purpose of reflection. If input from others is to be invited, you might then ask students to request a comment either from you or from another student, giving them practice at developing views to show others.

Microblogging (such as Twitter) provides a rapid response mechanism allowing multiple entries to be handled efficiently. It is suitable for field work or placement activities, or activities which require students to convey the 'gist' of an idea (such as a headline in a journalism subject) and attract the responses of others, but it does not allow for in-depth reflection.

Wikis

The central advantage of wikis, in terms of activities which involve creation of content, is that they provide a collaborative space in which a number of people can create content together. They also offer other advantages which we mentioned in Chapter 2, including a record of individual contributions, the ability to revert to previous versions of the work that is created, and a discussion space that is separate from the 'work space'.

While wikis are often used in ways that include the teacher's participation, in student group work they can be used to support the concept of learner control (Dron, 2007b), so that the wiki is 'owned' by the group. This may mean, as we noted previously, that you might need to provide considerable support (through dialogue and structure) *outside* the Web 2.0 environment to nurture the group process, but avoid interfering within it. When the link to the wiki is from a site on the LMS, the support information can be provided on this site. We recognise the conceptual contradiction of entering a user-controlled environment through the teacher-controlled gateway of a learning management system but this offers the advantage of a single access point to the online learning environment and a sense of all the components being part of a cohesive whole. An emerging issue related to student control is that as social software is added to the tools in learning management systems it becomes more difficult to distinguish these spaces as their own.

A useful strategy for supporting students and helping them to prepare for an activity in a wiki is to provide them initially with a simple task to complete in a 'practice wiki'. This can be important in gaining familiarity with the environment, and particularly in overcoming reluctance to edit each other's work.

For example ...

- Provide a wiki page that has been populated with 'poorly prepared' material that might include (obvious) factual errors, spelling and expression errors and disorganised sequencing of ideas. Ask the group to work together to improve it. If there is

---

> more than one group (each with its own wiki) use the same material in each wiki and then open the wikis to the other groups after the time allocated to the task is complete so that they can compare their efforts.
>
> *and/or*
>
> ■ Ask the group to complete a simple, authentic task such as compiling a list of rules for the group. Compilation of a list of some kind is useful because it involves: (1) generation of ideas; (2) evaluating them for appropriateness; and (3) placing items in a preferred order.

Shared documents

E-portfolios, blogs and wikis are useful if the output of student work is to be a web-based document. However, if the output is to be a text document, a spreadsheet or some other form of presentation that is not web-based, then students working in groups using shared documents such as Google Documents can have the advantage of working on the same document which remains on the server while the task is in progress, and then presenting the final 'product' in the format required.

Student podcasting

While lecturers often think of podcasting as something they can do themselves to provide content for their students, learning activities or assessment tasks that involve student podcasting provide an excellent way of engaging them in the creation of content. The video (or audio) format may be particularly suited to activities where students develop skills or put together visual content. Middleton (2009) provides examples of student involvement in the creation of podcasts which include:

■ nursing staff and students producing video learning objects about clinical techniques; and

■ journalism students working independently to create vox pops (as an essential journalism technique) with a range of people on the topic of 'What makes a good student?', and later creating a short feature on 'why you would study Journalism at the university' as a marketing device.

Thompson (2007) describes a 'Grammar in a Pod Project' used in the professional preparation of English language teachers as a means of creating a collective resource for teaching grammar in upper primary school classrooms. The trainees were tasked to create a three minute podcast to explicitly teach a point of grammar and to select a non-fiction text that modelled the use of the grammar point. This was combined with a self-reflection task and a peer review of another trainee's podcast, thereby combining authentic learning and assessment.

Specific advantages of student podcasting videos mostly relate to accessing authentic content and motivation. The podcast video is easily viewed via a browser by both students and staff, and student control of who has access can be a motivating factor. In the journalism example above, the technology of podcasting is used for real-world communication so both the process and the content contribute to the authenticity of the activity.

Mobile technologies

Just as mobile technologies offer advantages for interaction between users and interaction with content, they also have value in relation to creation of content through their ability to capture and share authentic artefacts. Aubusson, Schuck and Burden (2009) comment on the immediacy and spontaneity of capturing live events, and describe the potential for collaborative reflection that can result from sharing events and deconstructing them with critical friends. This has obvious advantages for some learning contexts and, of course, the mobile device can simply be used for capturing the data with sharing and discussion occurring after it has been downloaded.

* * *

Whatever the learning activities you provide for your students, consideration of the feedback that they will receive when they complete them is a design issue that is of critical importance for both guiding learning and offering support. Often the nature of the technology you are using will determine how this is done and its affordances will streamline the feedback process. In the following section we address some of the aspects of feedback that you should consider.

Giving activity feedback: principles, options and issues

Nicol and Macfarlane-Dick (2006, p. 205) suggest seven principles of good feedback practice, indicating that it:

1. helps clarify what good performance is (goals, criteria, expected standards);
2. facilitates the development of self-assessment (reflection) in learning;
3. delivers high quality information to students about their learning;
4. encourages teacher and peer dialogue around learning;
5. encourages positive motivational beliefs and self-esteem;
6. provides opportunities to close the gap between current and desired performance;
7. provides information to teachers that can be used to help shape teaching.

Feedback will usually be formalised when it occurs in conjunction with graded assessment tasks (which may be relevant if the learning activities that you design contribute directly to this assessment). However, ideally there will be plentiful opportunities for informal feedback prior to this and it is important that you make students aware that it can be provided in a variety of ways. *Explain how they will be receiving feedback so that they recognise it as such.* Emphasising the role of feedback from sources other than you can both reduce your own workload and provide direct benefits to learning. For example, Nicol and Macfarlane-Dick present their principles in the context of helping students to take control of their own learning and becoming self regulated learners by generating their own feedback. In addition, online communication can be valuable for supporting peer feedback. This has benefits for the student providing the feedback through the critical reflection involved, as well as for the student receiving the feedback who might then respond, and for others who observe or then build on the feedback that is generated. When students are working in groups, feedback to each other becomes a natural part of their engagement and learning as they work on a task together. Nevertheless, students often like to hear (virtually or otherwise) the voice of the teacher as well. Whatever you decide, make sure that you let students know exactly what to expect.

> ## For example ...
>
> In a discussion you might have two components to an activity. You might ask students to:
>
> - write a paragraph on a particular topic, then
> - critically comment on the contribution of another student.
>
> In the second of these activities you are asking students to give feedback to each other. You may need to be specific about what you mean by the term 'critically'. You may then further ask students to refine their original contribution in the light of the feedback they have received.
>
> It can often be helpful if you schedule specific dates for: (1) the initial contribution; (2) the critical contribution of another student; and (3) the date by which you respond after these two steps. However, you may need to decide whether to include the proviso that you will contribute earlier if guidance seems necessary.

Encouraging students to give and seek feedback can help them to become independent learners. Suggest sources of feedback to them. As well as each other, this could include family and friends (many of us would encourage students to get a friend to read an essay before submission), colleagues in their workplace or mentors both personal and professional. Often workplace supervision of students on vocational placements will be built into their study programme and it is important that they recognise that the feedback they receive from these supervisors and others in the workplace plays a vital role in their learning.

As for feedback that is provided in a formal assessment context, activity feedback should be *timely*, *informative* and *supportive*.

Timely feedback

A key benefit of the online environment for feedback is the ability to speed up its provision – this is instantaneous in the case of automated feedback which we will consider in Chapter 4. For other forms of feedback, make sure that your subject structure allows for and encourages the provision of prompt feedback. This may involve clearly communicating expectations to those who are providing feedback, which may include the students themselves. In cases where your own workload or that of others may delay feedback, make sure that this period is minimised and that you let students know when feedback can be expected.

Informative feedback

As the principles suggested by Nicol and Macfarlane-Dick (2006) indicate, feedback should convey specific information that is directed towards improvement of learning. Thus, any judgement (even 'Well done!') should refer to the reasons supporting the statement. When tasks are not well done, specific suggestions for improvement should be included.

Supportive feedback

The supportive role of feedback is also covered in Nicol and Macfarlane-Dick's principles (no. 5). In an online environment this is especially important because the isolation resulting from the separation between teacher and other students can cause considerable anxiety for students and the need for higher levels of reassurance than you might usually provide.

Developing your design

Once you have a clear idea of the kind of activities, resources and supports that you want to include in your online environment, you will need to think about how you will integrate them in that environment. How you do this will be determined to a large extent by whether you are planning a classroom-enhanced environment, a blended one of the type a, b or c in Figure 3.1, a completely online environment, or a variation of one of these.

Not only will you need to integrate activities, resources and supports, but also integrate modes of learning so that the online learning relates to the face-to-face learning (where applicable) and all relates to assessment, making sure students know where resources and support are, and when, where and how to access them.

Each of the types of learning environments shown in Figure 3.1 has its own issues in relation to development and implementation. A totally online environment with no opportunity to resolve difficulties face-to-face is often the most challenging. Table 3.4 covers some of the development issues related to each of these options.

Figure 3.1 Classroom-enhanced, blended and fully online learning designs

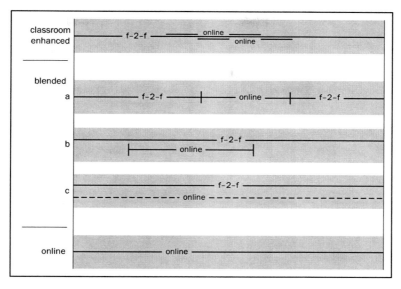

Table 3.4 Issues relating to online options

Mode	Description	Issues
Classroom-enhanced	The online environment is accessed during f-2-f sessions.	■ Is student input integral to their learning? ■ Will you use student input diagnostically?
Blended a	There are f-2-f phases and online phases but the two don't overlap; this might occur if students are on work placement for a period.	■ How are the two modes linked? ■ Are the phases dependent on each other? ■ Is guidance for the online phase given in the f-2-f session? ■ Are the same staff members involved in each? ■ Is assessment related to the online environment?
Blended b	There are continuous f-2-f sessions with the online environment supporting a particular activity.	■ The issues are generally as above.

(Continued)

Table 3.4   Issues relating to online options *(cont'd)*

Mode	Description	Issues
Blended c	The online environment is active throughout the teaching period, concurrent with the f-2-f environment.	■ What role does the online environment play, e.g., is it for support? ■ Are there specific activities associated with the online environment?
All online	Learning is totally online with no f-2-f components.	■ Is learning self-directed or is there interaction between students? ■ Are all resources online or is there a mix of paper and online resources? ■ What guidance will students need?

Now you can start planning the overall structure. Think about the following questions.

- What support will *you* need? You may need to have technical training, e.g., in the use of the LMS. Or you may need an expert developer, e.g., a web developer, multimedia or video developer. If you need to involve a developer you will probably need funding.

- Will you need to involve other teachers? If you teach with tutors you may need to involve them in the planning and implementation to ensure that the roles they undertake support your design.

- What timeframe will you need to consider? If you are planning a big project you might decide to incorporate a number of phases with trials, formalised evaluation procedures, and contingency planning.

There are a number of issues which may affect your planning. We have touched on some of them already but Table 3.5 provides a summary list for you to consider.

General student support issues

We have covered a number of issues and opportunities involving support in relation to learning activities throughout this chapter because the design of support for students is an intrinsic component of online learning design. We have also referred to support in guiding students to resources to encourage appropriate interaction with content. The guidance on

Table 3.5 Development issues

Time
Do you have time to develop what you have in mind? Remember that multimedia materials involve planning which requires considerable lead time.

Cost
Is there a cost involved and do you have funding to meet it?

Support
Do you need support and, if so, do you know where to obtain it? Are you able to participate in the teamwork that will be involved if you have experts in particular areas to assist you?

Accessibility
Do you know how to address accessibility issues relating to:
- online material?
- your particular student cohort (for example, particular needs of off-campus or international students in specific locations)?

Usability
Do you know how to design electronic learning materials that are easy for students to use?

Copyright
Do you know the copyright laws affecting you relating to use of third party materials (print and online)?

Internationalisation
How will you accommodate the needs of students from other countries and/ or non-English speaking backgrounds?

how to go about an activity, training in the use of technologies, and instructions required to complete it are all part of the support that you provide.

Think back to the characteristics of your students and the context of their learning and this will provide you with clues about the support facilities that you should provide as part of the design of your site. Once you have done this, the advantage of your site as a dynamic, living space, means that you can tailor more specific forms of support as you go along. Remember that if you are using transactional distance theory to guide your design, your use of dialogue and structure may be key components in planning the supports that you will provide.

As well as support that is specifically shaped to help students complete particular kinds of activities, at a more general level you will support students in knowing what to do and what is expected of them, and what they can expect from you, through different forms of guidance, announcements, schedules, etc. If you find that students often ask the same questions, you may need to compile some 'Frequently Asked Questions' to provide them with answers. Yet another level of support is usually provided at an institutional level and students may need to be reminded of this.

For example ...

Most institutions have a range of support services for students. They may include a 'helpdesk' for supporting their use of the learning management system, as well as other support services relating to library skills, academic skills, counselling, etc. Make sure that students know about these services and encourage their use, rather than asking you for help in these matters.

Any particular cohort of learners might also need specific support related to their circumstances. The characteristics of your students which we explored in Chapter 1 will help identify these needs.

For example ...

Mature age students may need support in logging into and using the LMS; another cohort of students might need learning skills support; yet others may need support in managing or organising groups or placements.

As part of this you will also need to consider their requirements in terms of technical support which we addressed in Chapter 2, building it in to your design as we discussed in relation to online communication earlier in this chapter. However, take care to avoid stereotyping (as we also mentioned in Chapter 2) and focus on the particular characteristics of your students that you have identified. Choosing a mode of communication with your students that is readily available, or with which they are familiar, has accessibility advantages. Mobile devices can be useful in this regard. As always, this will depend on the characteristics of your students.

> ### For example ...
>
> You may choose to use instant text messaging (SMS) by mobile phone to support them – e.g., to alert them to events, in addition to the pedagogical uses we considered earlier.

Many students are familiar with text messaging and may support each other in this way, whether or not you are involved. In deciding about your involvement think carefully about how integral this is to the learning experience. If you encourage students to contact you for support, will they develop an over reliance on you and under utilise the resources and support in their placement environment? Or will your support be a lifeline for students in unfamiliar and unsupportive environments? You will need to consider the workload both for you and for students if you build mobile communication into support arrangements.

Managing and administering online learning

You will have been aware as we considered the design of different kinds of activities and resources, that the management of these components may have major implications for your workload, both in setting up your online environment and then in running it. A considerable proportion of this will involve management of the aspects of support that we have discussed.

Managing discussion moderation

When you are running activities through online discussion the role of e-moderation in 'chairing' or managing the discussion in ways that will guide learning can be very time consuming if you don't plan it carefully. This is usually the role of the teacher or tutor but, as we discussed earlier, it can also be a valuable role for students to play (on an allocated basis) which will help them focus on shaping a particular discussion to meet the learning objectives for which it was designed.

As we also indicated earlier in this chapter, the initial goal of e-moderation is to welcome and encourage students, and to facilitate socialisation in establishing a learning environment. We noted in Chapter 2 that online discussion rarely occurs spontaneously. There are many examples of teaching staff providing discussion forums which students never use. The success of an un-moderated discussion depends on its purpose and the characteristics of participants. You can influence the outcome of the discussion by knowing the characteristics of your students and what motivates them. The socialisation stage is a good time to find out more about your students. Ultimately, you will need to weigh up the advantages and disadvantages of providing an un-moderated discussion topic. Often this will depend on whether you are providing the discussion space primarily for learning activities, support or social purposes.

Managing time

One of the major concerns that staff often have about teaching online is the time involved. Online activities which require feedback to individual students from you will require commitment of time, whether it is an activity based on a quiz format, a discussion, or a web editing application (e.g., blog or wiki). The timing of the workload depends on the application. For example, designing a quiz with feedback on each alternative question response requires an upfront investment of time, whereas the timing of feedback for discussion or collaborative activities will depend upon when students are completing them. Working in the online environment can easily take much more time than you realise or intend, so you may need to develop strategies to accommodate this. For example, set aside certain time periods each week for your online teaching, or try to complete most of the development work outside teaching periods (easier said than done!).

In managing online discussions there are a number of strategies that can help you to manage your time.

> ## For example ...
>
> - Specify at the beginning of the teaching period at what points you will respond, and to what extent.
> - Send a 'global' response to student activities rather than responding to individual contributions.

- Schedule 'guest moderators', such as outside experts, to moderate discussion on topics that are related to their expertise.
- Organise students to undertake specific tasks such as e-moderation (as mentioned previously), or giving feedback, or various group roles.

Your students will also face some time-related issues which you need to manage.

For example ...

- Are your students in a different time zone? This might make synchronous online activities impossible (for example, chat sessions, videoconferences), and can introduce extra time delays for responses in asynchronous discussion forums. This also has implications if you are setting times and due dates for submission of work online. You may need to alert your students if submission times relate to your home campus, or provide different submission times for students in different time zones.

- When designing online activities, consider how long it will take for everyone (both your students and any teaching staff) to complete what is required. If you want your students to participate in an active discussion on a particular question, you need to consider how often each student accesses the unit and how long it takes for several students to respond to the question. Even if students regularly log in two to three times per week, it can take two weeks for a topic to be discussed. Compare this to what you might achieve in a face-to-face tutorial.

- To ensure that students do not become excessively and unproductively involved in a particular discussion, you may need to provide prompts about where they should be up to, or even close off some discussion topics after a suitable time has elapsed.

Many of these considerations apply equally to any online activity where students make contributions. Students creating e-portfolios, blogs or wikis may want individual feedback on their work to ensure they are on the 'right track' before proceeding further.

Managing expectations

Managing student expectations is another important aspect of teaching online.

- **Be clear what you expect from your students:** What are you hoping your students will gain from engaging in a particular activity? Is it necessary that they all actively participate? In a discussion activity, are you going to allow students to just read postings from others ('lurking')? It may be that reading all postings will achieve the same learning outcomes for shy students, as active participation in the discussion will achieve for more outgoing students. The resolution of this issue will depend on the purpose of the discussion in relation to learning and assessment.

  Do you require all online engagement to be related to the unit content, or will you allow students to communicate with each other on other topics?

For example ...

If the discussion space is designed for a specific activity then the objectives of that activity may indicate that students are to develop and demonstrate critical skills. In this case you would expect each student to contribute. If, on the other hand, the discussion space is to support students then it may not matter if they do not contribute. In this case several students may have similar difficulties and your response to one discussion post may offer effective support to other students without the need for them to contribute.

You may like to provide areas where students can post messages about difficulties with technology, particularly if they are becoming distressed or frustrated with accessing parts of the unit. Students may not always articulate their distress about technology, and may feel that they are the only ones suffering a particular problem.

- **Be clear what your students can expect from you:** Are you going to respond to all questions within a specified time frame? Are you simply going to monitor all student activities, and correct only any misinformation that is posted? Or are you going to refrain from responding for a specified period, and encourage others to respond?

  Students often complete their online work late at night or at weekends, so providing prompt feedback is obviously unrealistic (but some may still expect it!). You might give an undertaking to answer questions or provide feedback within two or three working days.

  If you prefer to encourage students to answer questions posted by their peers, you will need to make this expectation clear. Perhaps you could commit to providing feedback after seven days, to allow sufficient time for students to read the question, and undertake some research if necessary. Maybe a 'reward' could be offered for the best student answer.

- **Set clear rules and standards for discussion postings:** A basic expectation you may need to communicate to students is the style and standard of their online contributions. If the purpose of communication is peer support, informal language may be appropriate, but for communication associated with learning activities a more formal style may be needed. However, it is important not to expect students to write 'essays' in discussion spaces – the style of communication needs to fit the medium and the characteristics of the tool. While online discussions are text-based, they have many of the characteristics of verbal communication. Online communications cannot take advantage of facial and bodily cues, so using an appropriate 'tone of voice' in messages is important.

For example ...

It is easy for some forms of humour to be misinterpreted when facial expressions are unseen. In such cases use of the keyboard to represent emotions (emoticons) can be helpful, for example: ☺, ☹.

Depending upon your students' experience of learning in the online environment, you may need to specify some basic rules of netiquette.

Managing large groups

If you have a large cohort of students, you will usually need to divide them into groups to manage online activities effectively. This raises the question of how you manage each group. While the 'global' response mentioned earlier is one option (and this could be offered in a general discussion space which is open to all), it will often be more beneficial in terms of feedback to students if you (or someone else) can be responsible for managing students at the group level.

For example ...

You could assign small groups to be the 'experts' on a given topic, required to post a question, lead the discussion and, at the end of the week, summarise the major points for the whole class. You could then respond to the final summary.

Managing difficult situations

Smooth running of an online class requires good communication skills both written and oral, including 'listening'. Despite good intentions, difficult situations can arise in handling students with poor communication skills. Maintaining boundaries is central to dealing with these situations.

Recognising poor communication behaviour early can help keep a student (or a group of students) on track. Poor communication skills can also result in silence, and this is difficult to distinguish from those who are 'lurking' in online discussion. It may mean that students are having problems, or that they are reluctant to communicate either in a 'public' discussion space or privately with you, or there may be some other reason.

For example ...

You might deal with students who are silent in a discussion by directing questions to them. Alternatively, you might engage them privately (by email) to explore the reasons for their silence.

If the activities are well aligned with the objectives and assessment, the problem of non-participation should not occur, particularly if the activities form part of the assessment. However, you may still need to provide support to guide students in participating appropriately.

Illustrating the ideas in this chapter ...

On the following pages, Suzy continues her story to illustrate how she addressed aspects of online design and development.

Suzy's story continued ...

Because planning my online learning design began with the idea of an assessment task that would allow students to meet some specific learning objectives, one of the basic principles of constructive alignment was already there. I then had to decide what students needed to do to help them complete that task, and how I would design and manage the resources and support they needed.

There were some important theoretical perspectives that helped me. I had realised that social constructivist principles based on Vygotsky (1978) were influential in online learning, just as they had been influential in guiding my own work. However, while I found descriptions of the social situation of learning useful, they did not necessarily account for how online learning frames the capacity for assessment to be used as a context for teaching. Then I was lucky enough to attend the 2009 Vygotsky Summer School in Belya Kalitiva, Russia, run by Vygotsky's granddaughter (Elena Kravtsova) and I saw how Vygotsky's work had been developed by his students El'konin and Davydov, and later further developed by their students, Kravtsov and Kravtsova (2009). This includes use of the following three stages:

1. a learning activity as a 'leading activity' for reflection;
2. the learning actions by which the learner engages with the learning task; and
3. a structural component that involves sharing mastery of the completed task in a given social situation.

I used this staged approach in my design, which involved a blended online learning environment since my students were studying on-campus. At Stage 1, students preparing digital responses used online resources (e.g., online lectures on the LMS, digital copies of readings, lectures on YouTube, podcasts) to access theoretical content for completing their responses. At Stage 2, they completed the response, and at Stage 3 they demonstrated and discussed how the theory was situated within their practice.

To achieve this, I asked students (in groups of three or four) to prepare one digital response per week over the first five weeks of semester (each response relating to the content for that week). This preparation was undertaken during the weekly tutorial, which provided the major opportunity for feedback and support, helping them to develop their ideas before participating in a three-week practicum which followed the five-week period. At the end of each of the five weeks I asked students to post their digital response on the LMS site under the relevant link for their group. Prior to attending the next class they viewed each posting and decided which response they thought most accurately summarised the content for that week. During class I asked them to contribute to a secret ballot in which they (individually) voted for their preferred posting. This provided additional feedback, while the practicum itself was a key source of feedback through the experience it offered.

Two weeks after their practicum, I asked students to:

1. Select three of their best/most interesting/preferred digital responses from weeks 1 to 5.

2. Compose these so that they were presented as one file (e.g., PowerPoint, Word).

3. For each of the selected digital responses, justify why they included it in their presentation based on the following criteria:

   - the significance of the topic for their understanding about how infants and toddlers learn/grow, and how quality care can best be provided for young children; and

   - what they learned about the topic in relation to the practice of quality care giving by developing the digital response.

4. Conclude the presentation with a short discussion/reflection on the process involved in doing the digital responses – what

they found beneficial, what was frustrating, what amendments should be made to the process/assignment in the future, etc.

Once this scheduling was established, there were no management or administrative issues that could not be dealt with during the weekly class. Because of the authentic nature of the activity, which involved the creation of an assessment item, students were motivated and enthusiastic.

Figure 3.2 shows an example of a digital response provided by one of the groups. This group decided to represent a not-for-profit organisation against childhood consumerism titled 'Keep It Real Kids' (KIRK). Each week their digital response challenged dominant conceptions of children and childhood in the media.

Summary

This chapter has covered some of the key issues that you will need to consider as you begin to design your online learning environment. It has introduced some additional theories and models that might help to guide your design. We have addressed the alignment of learning objectives, activities and assessment, noting the value of merging learning activities and assessment, and of using activities as the starting point of your design, to help students meet the relevant objectives. We have focused particularly on activities that involve communication and/or collaboration among users, and those that involve interaction with or creation of content, in each case highlighting the importance of designing appropriate resources and supports to assist students in the completion of the activities. We then noted some of the issues that you might need to consider in developing your design, and commented on general student support, management and administrative issues that may be relevant in implementing it. We hope you now recognise the extent to which you will need to reconceptualise your face-to-face teaching or assessment practices in the online environment.

Design and development for teaching in an online environment can be quite challenging when you do it for the first time so we would again encourage you to start with something small and simple, if possible. You should regard this as an iterative process that will evolve as you gain experience of teaching or assessing online, drawing on the feedback that you receive. It is also advisable to evaluate progressively during design

Figure 3.2 An example of a digital response by a student group

Keep It Real Kids
Letting kids be kids. Not a consumerist body.

- Home
- Events Calender
- Members Login

About KIRK
- Our Mission
- Issues facing children and families
- Latest News
- Contact Us
- Subscribe to Newsletter

KIRK Programs
- Upcoming seminars
- Online Chat
- Annual conference
- Project Sheets NEW!

Useful WebPages
- Early Childhood Australia
- Government educational site
- Junior Bees
- Kid Spot

Home | Events Calender | Mission | Contact Us
© 2008 Keep It Real Kids (KIRK) | Privacy and Disclaimer
ABN 31 930 635 743
PO Box 52 Idealistic Lane Vic 3199
Tel: (03) 5971 7585 | Fax: 9571 7584
Email: kirk@bigpond.com.au

Site by KIRK

We are a parent body who felt the need to inform others of the concerns parents face when influenced by widely accepted opinions and views on early childhood.

Our Mission

K.I.R.K is a non-profit organization committed to educating and promoting an image of the child that moves away from consumerist marketing.

Inform the community of the foundations of early childhood including the importance of the images of children, brain development, interactions and relationships.

To provide information to parents, guardians, carers and extended community based on scholarly research.

Latest News

On the 31st of July following our appearance on Channel 7 Sunrise show, we had a follow up real time chat on *Interactions and Relationships with toddlers and infants*. Our special guest was professor Carly Dickenson. To read the extract of this informative discussion click here: Chat Link

Have you seen our latest tools for creating your own play experiences in the home? We have just developed a set of project sheets demonstrating ways of incorporating old and used items from around the home, and turning them into entertaining children's toys. You can find these on our webpage.

 On September 12th we are holding a seminar on *Playing to learn in infant and toddler programs*. The guest speaker is Dr. Susan Edwards, a renowned lecturer at Monash University.

Information of this seminar can be found here: Seminar Link

and development as this will guide you even before you have offered your online environment for the first time. We will consider some strategies for doing this in Chapter 5. You will develop numerous ideas for adjusting your design from your first experience of online teaching, both through formal evaluation processes and the experience itself. This will help you to finetune aspects of the environment to achieve a better fit with your students' characteristics and your learning and teaching context. It may also alert you to support, management and administrative issues that you will need to address (and, in fact, found you had to address during the first iteration) but did not initially consider.

In Chapter 4 we will focus specifically on online assessment design and implementation which, as we have said previously, will involve some overlap with this chapter because of the links between objectives, activities and assessment.

The checklist which you began in Chapters 1 and 2 continues below. It covers the aspects of design and development we have addressed in this chapter. If you are able to answer 'Yes' to most questions here, you should have a good initial sense of what is involved in online design, development and implementation even though you are likely to refine those ideas later. If your answer to most questions is 'No' it may be helpful to try and locate as many examples of online learning design as you can (within your institution or beyond), especially designs that are helping students to meet the kinds of learning objectives that you have in mind. Seek out sources of academic professional development if you have not done so before and try to identify successful online teachers. Talk to them, find out what they do, and get their advice on the opportunities and challenges. And remember to start with a small and simple online component if you possibly can.

Are you able to identify ...	Yes	Unsure	No
15. Any additional theories or models that will help to guide your online learning design?			
16. How you will align the objectives that are driving your online learning design with appropriate learning activities and assessment tasks?			

Are you able to identify ...	Yes	Unsure	No
17. The kinds of activities that you will design involving interaction between users, interaction with content and/or creation of content?			
18. The kinds of specific learning resources and supports that you will need to design for the activities you plan to develop?			
19. Issues that you may face in developing your design and how you will address them?			
20. General student support issues you will need to consider in designing your environment and how you will address them?			
21. The management and administrative issues that you may need to deal with as you begin to implement specific aspects of your design (e.g., online discussion groups or Web 2.0 spaces such as blogs or wikis), and strategies for dealing with them?			
22. Any other factors that you may need to consider in designing or developing your online environment? (Specify below.)			

Note

1. Activities such as these are similar to those that we have included as interactions with the computer interface in Chapter 4 but we have referred to them here because their emphasis is on learning rather than assessment.

Online assessment

Introduction

We noted in Chapter 3 the close relationship between the design of online learning activities and assessment tasks, and the advantages of merging activities and assessment where this is possible. Hence, we have already considered some ideas that are important in online assessment, including the alignment of objectives, activities and assessment, and the role of feedback in supporting and extending learning opportunities. We will now explore in more detail some of the multiple reasons and opportunities for assessing online, and some of the challenges you might face.

Making decisions about whether, when or how to use online assessment in your teaching requires a clear focus on the nature and purposes of assessment and on the basic principles of assessment design. It also requires you to know about the affordances of the online technologies that are available to you, which you considered in Chapter 2. We will begin by reviewing some general characteristics of assessment in higher education, then introduce some of the common uses of the online environment for assessment, and identify some opportunities and challenges of these uses that you might consider. We will also address ways of implementing assessment practices online and deal with some of the support, management and administrative issues that arise if you are planning online assessment.

We proceed from the assumption that assessment should only occur online if this *benefits*, or *does not inhibit*, student learning. The latter point is important because online assessment offers a number of administrative benefits (for the student and/or the teacher), as well as benefits to learning, and it is important to consider these. However, we support the view that an administrative benefit should not be accompanied by a cost in terms of student learning. In this topic we focus mainly on considerations about assessment which relate to student learning.

We begin by reviewing some key understandings about the nature and purposes of assessment to provide a context for the kinds of opportunities offered by online assessment.

Why assess?

When we think of assessment we often think of examinations and assignments, of grading the performance of students in order to decide if they should 'pass' a particular subject or part of it. But assessment reaches beyond grading, and online assessment helps us to extend that reach, not only by facilitating the assessment process but also by opening up possibilities that are not available in the face-to-face environment.

Ramsden (2003) summarises some of the important contemporary themes relating to the role of assessment in higher education. As a central assumption, he draws on the view of assessment expressed by Rowntree (1977) which we mentioned in Chapter 1. This suggests that assessment is an interaction which is aimed, to some extent, at knowing another person. The view that assessment is about more than the measurement of performance has become influential in recent years. Serafini (2004) identified three paradigms of assessment: assessment as measurement; followed historically by assessment as procedure; and thirdly, assessment as inquiry. The idea of assessment as inquiry has led to a focus on its value for learning, rather than being 'primarily about the allocation of rewards and punishments' (Ramsden, 2003, p. 180). Hence, the distinction is often made between formative assessment *for* learning (e.g., Boud, 1995, 2007; Carless, 2007), assessment *of* learning (summative assessment), and assessment *as* learning, 'when students personally monitor what they are learning and use the feedback from this monitoring to make adjustments, adaptations, and even major changes in what they understand ... [which] is the ultimate goal where students are their own best assessors' (Earl, 2003, p. 25).

The aspects of feedback that we considered in Chapter 3 illustrate characteristics of formative assessment. Gibbs, Habeshaw and Habeshaw (1988, p. 7) explained the *formative* and *summative* components of assessment as follows:

> Assessing is a general term used to describe all those activities and processes involved in judging performance. Assessing can be summative or formative: summative assessment is concerned with a

final judgement of performance; formative assessment is concerned with the improvement of performance. In broad terms *marking* and *grading* involve summative assessment while *reviewing* and *giving feedback* involve formative assessment.

For example ...

- You may want to know how learners are progressing towards the outcomes specified by the learning objectives so you can target your teaching effectively at either group or individual level. You can make a *formative assessment* of how learners are responding to the activities you have designed, by looking at their input and/or asking them questions about problems they may have. You will then be able to give learners feedback, as we discussed in Chapter 3, which helps them get over hurdles and resolve difficulties. As well as supporting their learning this will give you ideas about teaching strategies you might implement to address any problems they are having.

- If you want evidence of students' learning in a subject in order to give them a score for their achievements, you might use a variety of assessment tasks (some of which we will consider in this chapter), including formal examinations. The learning objectives often determine the most appropriate form of the assessment tasks. The combined grades from these tasks would then be used for a final judgement of performance (summative assessment), usually as students complete their study of a subject.

Within these two purposes of assessment, further distinctions can be made. Among the many reasons for assessment Crooks (1988) listed the following as relevant in higher education:

1. selection and placement;
2. motivation;
3. focusing learning – the 'hidden curriculum';
4. consolidating and structuring learning;
5. guiding and correcting learning;
6. determining readiness to proceed;

7. certifying or grading achievement; and

8. evaluating teaching.

Your own reasons for assessing students may vary from those listed, but note how all but the last of these are aspects of either formative assessment (which deal with guiding the learning of students through providing support and feedback) or summative assessment (those that are concerned with summarising and confirming past achievement). Because the formative role of assessment has most direct influence on the process of student learning, making sure you have considered this carefully will give you more options to consider about how you might assess online.

For example ...

- Contributions to online discussions provide opportunities for feedback from you or from other students in the class.
- Online formative assessment quizzes are easy for students to undertake, in their own time, as many times as they need to, offering immediate feedback which you have designed as part of the test.

A part of formative assessment involves identifying students' prior knowledge and skills in order to clarify the aspects of their performance which you (and they) will need to focus on. *Diagnostic assessment* is often used at the beginning of a teaching period for this purpose and to help you find out more about the characteristics of your students so that you can provide the support they need to achieve the intended learning outcomes.

For example ...

You could:

- set a pre-test with incorporated feedback (which is matched with a later post-test to identify the learning that has occurred);
- ask students to write a letter or reflection about themselves and their learning;

> - ask students to complete a self assessment task in which they evaluate their past learning; or
>
> - provide a brief questionnaire on issues related to students' goals, expectations, potential problems, etc.
>
> **Note:** The use of audience response systems or networked tablet computers in a classroom-enhanced context provides excellent opportunities for diagnostic assessment and formative guidance and feedback at a class level.

You might be concerned about the extra workload that these different forms of assessment could have for you, but there are many ways of managing assessment and the online environment can help you to do this. Distributing the workload is one option. The question of 'who assesses?' has quite a few implications for assessment in the online environment.

Who assesses?

The traditional answer to the above question is you (the teacher), or tutors, or markers whom you pay to do the job. This may be relevant for much of the summative assessment of your students but it ignores important opportunities in assessment for learning. Identifying others who are able to contribute to assessment can help you to deal with workload, help students to take responsibility for their own learning, and has the potential to bring in new perspectives, e.g., from experts. You may already be implementing self or peer assessment which raises the possibility of encouraging students to be assessors and opening up to them the additional learning possibilities associated with the assessment role.

Self assessment

Self assessment encourages students to become active, independent learners and contribute to the generation of feedback for themselves, helping to prepare them for life after university. Boud (1991, p. 5) states that self assessment is about the involvement of students in:

- identifying standards and/or criteria to apply to their work and
- making judgements about the extent to which they have met these criteria and standards.

He goes on to say:

> Self assessment means more than students grading their own work; it means involving them in the processes of determining what is good work in any given situation. They are required to consider what are the characteristics of, say, a good essay or practical report and to apply this to their own work.

As we have already noted, aspects of the online environment that support reflection, including e-portfolios, blogs, and online discussion, can be very helpful in encouraging self assessment.

Peer assessment

Roberts (2006, p. 6) defines peer assessment as 'the process of having the learners critically reflect upon, and perhaps suggest grades for, the learning of their peers'.

For example ...

You may ask students to assess the individual work of one of their peers by critiquing the work of a partner and giving them feedback and, perhaps, a grade.

Although there are valuable learning opportunities in asking students to assess the work of their peers, there are common problems associated with summative peer assessment. These include collusion, reluctance to participate and friendship bias, as well as effects of gender, age, ability or ethnicity. Strategies such as requiring students to justify ratings, and explicitly linking criteria with ratings, can address a number of these problems (Falchikov, 2005). When using peer assessment summatively it is better to use an overall global mark with well-understood criteria, and to involve students in discussions about criteria, than to ask them to rate many individual dimensions (Falchikov, 2005).

A number of software programs have been specifically designed to implement structured peer assessment online and support the provision of feedback and grades by students. See Tucker, Fermelis and Palmer (2009), Raban and Litchfield (2007) or Sung, Chang, Chiou and Hou (2005) for some recent examples. You would be unlikely to consider one of these if you were embarking on online assessment unless a similar system already exists at your institution. At a simpler level, your learning management system may provide customisable grading forms which you can use to support reliability and validity in the context of peer assessment.

Other assessors

Other potential assessors include mentors (formal or informal) and clinical or workplace supervisors or experts. Feedback from such people can increase authenticity of assessment and the online environment facilitates their input.

For example ...

- By inviting an expert (from anywhere in the world) to moderate an online discussion on a particular topic, students are able to benefit from 'real-world' experience and receive useful feedback. While this will relieve you of the demands of responding to students during this period you will still need to monitor the discussion in the context of the subject as a whole. The assessment task may include designing questions for the expert which could contribute to summative assessment.

- Clinical or workplace supervisors will provide invaluable formative assessment for students. As well as structured assessment events, make sure your students take advantage of the informal assessment that can be provided by such supervisors.

Some aspects of assessment design

In this section we will consider some important aspects of assessment design. These apply whether or not you are assessing online, but we will focus on those which have particular relevance in the online environment.

We addressed some of them in Chapter 3 when we considered the alignment of objectives, activities and assessment, including the benefits of merging learning tasks and assessment tasks (Oliver & Herrington, 2001), and when we noted the value of *authentic* learning tasks. We cover these points again here because of their importance to assessment. As in all design for online learning and assessment, an awareness of student characteristics and the learning and teaching context is an essential starting point.

Accommodating the learning and teaching context

Accommodating the learning and teaching context in assessment involves considering factors such as:

- the level of study (to determine the extent of guidance and structure that you need to provide);
- whether your assessment tasks accommodate different learning styles and abilities;
- whether the workload is appropriate; and
- whether the assessment is fair and offers equal opportunity to all students. This may include determining whether you have provided sufficient choice to accommodate different backgrounds and experiences (including different cultural backgrounds).

Depending on the learning outcome that is being assessed, in many circumstances a valuable way of acknowledging the student's context is to incorporate it in the assessment task. This has added advantages in terms of authenticity and it reduces the likelihood of plagiarism because the task is individualised.

For example ...

If you are teaching a community welfare subject you could ask students to complete a project which involved collection of information about community support services in their area and make some recommendations about improvements that are required, in the context of policies or theoretical perspectives covered in the subject.

Depending on the nature of the assessment, you may also need to consider factors such as access, costs and ethical issues.

> **For example ...**
>
> For the project above, you may need to facilitate students' access to appropriate support services and there may be ethical issues in collecting sensitive data that require approval. There could be costs involved if students need to travel to collect the information. You might also need to consider technology access in relation to submission of projects, depending on the way you wanted students to present evidence of the information they had collected.

Aligning objectives, activities and assessment

Whether or not learning activities are formally included as part of the summative assessment, they should always underpin assessment in some way to allow students to practise and demonstrate the kind of learning specified by the learning objectives. This alignment then also needs to be evident in the summative assessment task.

Designing authentic assessment tasks

Authentic assessment places value on both the process and the product of learning and provides added motivational benefits for students in terms of interest and relevance (avoiding the traditional assignment plus examination combination!). It is particularly applicable to online assessment because the environment offers affordances and tools to complete tasks in authentic ways and the process, as well as the product, is visible to the assessor.

> **For example ...**
>
> To assess knowledge of terms and definitions in a particular subject area you could ask students to build a glossary in a wiki, where they identify terms and contribute specific definitions and

> examples. This would provide a more authentic assessment task than the use of multiple choice or matching questions.

Mathur and Murray (2006, p. 256) have developed a useful checklist to determine the authenticity of an online assessment strategy. See Table 4.1.

Table 4.1	Checklist to determine the authenticity of an online assessment strategy

- Is the assessment strategy fair to students of all ethnic, language, colour, and gender based groups?
- Does the assessment strategy link content with students' authentic needs?
- Does the assessment strategy adequately demonstrate the student's ability to solve real life problems/situations?
- Does the assessment strategy provide sufficient time to complete the authentic task?
- Is the assessment strategy guided by student competency at entry point of the curriculum?
- Is the assessment strategy flexible and adaptable in that it can be modified if the context of learning changes?
- Does the assessment include a combination of strategies?
- Does the assessment strategy raise questions that have more than one correct solution?
- Is there provision for multiple raters?
- Does the assessment strategy provide a built-in mechanism for adequate and timely feedback?
- Are the assessment strategies described in a way that is understandable to the student and other raters?
- Is the authentic assessment strategy co-created by the instructor and the student?
- Does the authentic assessment strategy serve as a motivator for learning?

Source: Mather and Murray, 2006, p. 256.

While this list is not specific to the online environment, it provides a way to ensure the authenticity of your assessment design.

Designing group assessment

Group work is increasingly valued in higher education because it allows students to practise the kind of team-based tasks that they will encounter in the workplace; hence, it lends itself to authentic assessment. These activities provide immediate opportunities for formative peer assessment. This may be implicit in the design of the activity (through students negotiating), or you might explicitly request it. However, students often dislike summative assessment of group work when it does not recognise their individual contributions. Drawing on previous work, Falchikov (2005) discusses eight commonly used strategies for differentiating group and individual marks:

- multiplying the group mark by an individual weighting factor;
- distribution of a pool of marks;
- use of a contribution mark;
- separation of product and process;
- equally sharing a mark but with exceptional tutor intervention;
- splitting group tasks and individual tasks;
- issuing yellow (warning) and red (zero grade) cards to individuals perceived as not 'pulling their weight'; and
- calculating individual grades in terms of deviations from the norm.

Peer assessment, where each member of the group 'rates' contributions of other members, has also been used to address the issue of equity but concerns are often expressed about assessing individual contributions fairly (James, McInnes & Devlin, 2002). The strategy of using peer assessment summatively remains unreliable despite procedures designed to reduce bias (Kennedy, 2005; Li, 2001). Engaging students in discussion about the selected strategies provides an avenue to enhance peer assessment of group work with potential benefits for reliability and validity.

Linking formative and summative assessment

Students are often anxious about assessment, especially in the online environment when they are unfamiliar with the technology. In a totally online environment they may feel inhibited in asking for clarification. They may need more support than you are accustomed to providing but early, effective support through formative or low-stakes assessment can assist students in preparing for major summative assessment tasks.

It is desirable for learning if you design summative assessment tasks which also have a formative aspect so that you provide students with feedback, as well as a grade. In doing this, it is important that you make the most of these formative opportunities to guide learning and offer support, while providing a rationale for the grade.

For example ...

Consider the following points for structuring individual student comments.

- Begin with a positive, supportive statement. Even if the student has not successfully addressed a topic, it is possible to make a comment which establishes rapport, and emphasises the support available to deal with difficulties.

- Follow this with well organised, specific information on aspects which have been dealt with well, and constructive advice for addressing problem areas.

- Try to end with a positive, forward-looking statement which reinforces avenues for further help, if necessary.

As we discussed in Chapter 3, remember to offer feedback to students who are performing well, not only to those who need help. The above example combines informative feedback with acknowledgement feedback. The latter without the former type of feedback is of limited value for learning.

Scheduling assessment tasks carefully

In linking formative and summative assessment, scheduling plays an important part in assessment design. It has increased impact in a fully online environment when communication around assessment tasks may be the main form of contact you have with your students. Establish regular contact related to assessment beginning with an early diagnostic task.

For example ...

- Set an early diagnostic assessment task to make contact with students, determine their needs, and provide an opportunity for early guidance and feedback. This will help to develop students'

---

confidence, establish a relationship with them, and provide some early direction for future assignments. If you have a large enrolment, devise a task which does not require a lengthy comment, and to which you can respond on a simple marking form designed to fulfil the role of providing feedback. Speed up your feedback by responding online.

- Schedule assignments throughout the semester so that there are opportunities for progressive feedback and *ensure that you provide feedback well before the next assignment is due.*

- Where possible, try and ensure that the tasks you set do not clash with assessment tasks for other, related subjects.

Although it is important that students receive early feedback, it is helpful if early assessment tasks have minimum summative weighting while the students are becoming familiar with requirements. Providing quality feedback while minimising assignment turnaround times can be a difficult balance to achieve (though we have already mentioned some options in relation to 'who assesses?' and more will emerge as we consider some of the online options).

Continuous assessment, through a set of assessment tasks (preferably interlinked) is much better for learning than many of the alternatives, and it is another strategy which reduces opportunities for plagiarism. It can also contribute to validity of authentic assessment tasks which are individualised for students. However, it does present some challenges in terms of management. It means continuous time spent assessing rather than the 'one-hit' of marking an assignment or examination. While continuous assessment is valuable, *take care not to over-assess*, as that will have negative consequences for both you and your students. All you need is an appropriate sample of student learning that reflects the unit objectives.

For example ...

In a project with several parts, asking students to provide an outline of one part might be sufficient to determine how they are progressing and give them effective feedback for developing the assessment task further.

Using assessment criteria for grading assignments

Criterion-referenced assessment (where grades are allocated against assessment criteria which are determined by the learning objectives) provides more opportunities for improving learning than *normative assessment* (where grades are distributed according to a normal curve). It is helpful to both markers and students if assessment criteria are included on a marking form. You need to decide whether to design a *rubric* (grading scheme) for this purpose. Assessment rubrics can be very useful for summative assessment as they help describe what is expected and how each element (objective) will be rated. However, in some cases they can 'normalise' grades, and inhibit creativity. Students may consider the rubric as a list of boxes to be ticked rather than treating the assessment task as an opportunity for learning (Panko, 2006). An example of a rubric is provided in Figure 4.1.

Figure 4.1 Example of a rubric in a spreadsheet format

	A	B	C	D	E	F	G
1	Student:		Tutor:				
2	Mark	4	3	2	1	0	Mark
3	Report content						
4	Defining terms and contexts,	Clear, concise, relevant and comprehensive	Mostly clear, concise, relevant and comprehensive	Generally relevant, some parts obscurely expressed	Less than half relevant terms included, some irrelevant, some obscurely expressed	Most missing and/or obscurely or verbosely expressed	
5	Developing and supporting arguments	Covered all key points clearly, informative, appropriately referenced	Covered most key points clearly, generally well referenced	About half the key points covered, key references missing	Key points but lacking balance, few references	Few key points covered, no reference material	
6	Conclusions and recommendations	Conclusions clearly stated and put into context, relevant recommendations clearly expressed and justified (in terms of conclusions)	Conclusions mostly clearly stated and most put into context, some recommendations clearly expressed and justified	Key conclusions missing, recommendations not justified	Scant conclusions out of context, recommendations not justified	No conclusions, no recommendations	
7	Report style						
8	Layout (headings etc),	Well structured, relevant title and headings, creatively presented	Clearly set out with mostly relevant headings	Key headings missing, structure unclear	Structure and headings obscure,	No headings, obscure structure and flow	
9	Language, grammar, punctuation, spelling,	Well written, excellent expression, concise, clear	Mostly clear and well written, some parts verbose	Some parts difficult to understand	Some parts difficult to understand, several errors in spelling, expression, punctuation	Difficult to understand, many errors in spelling, expression, punctuation	
10	Bibliographic citation (style, accuracy)	Excellent reference list appropriately cited	Generally well referenced, most cited appropriately	Some references, some cited incorrectly	Few references, mostly cited incorrectly	No references	
11						TOTAL/24	

report rubric / presentation-rubric / project-rubric

If there is potential to negotiate assessment criteria for specific assignments with students within the scope of the objectives, this can provide a further assessment role they can undertake to benefit their learning.

For example ...

Involving students, either individually or as a group, in negotiation of a learning contract which includes the objectives, the assessment task/s and assessment criteria helps students understand how they will be assessed.

Engaging students in the assessment process can be a motivating strategy as well as a learning opportunity for them. As they learn more about assessment as a process there is the potential for them to develop self assessment skills which are critical for lifelong learning.

Considering reliability and validity

For summative assessment purposes, you need to design tasks so that assessment is:

- *reliable* – marking is consistent each time the task is administered; and
- *valid* – it gives you the best evidence possible of the abilities being examined.

You may need to implement measures to ensure that items can be consistently and objectively assessed, especially if there are multiple markers. Attention to assessment criteria and rubrics should help you to meet this requirement. It is also important to ensure that appropriate weighting, which reflects the specified objectives, is given to components within assessment tasks and across the range of assessment tasks that you provide.

A further issue to consider is that traditional notions of reliability and validity are challenged by recent developments in thinking about assessment that support authenticity and emphasise the highly contextualised nature of learning involved in preparing students for life and work. Boud and Falchikov (2006) comment on the socially constructed, highly situated nature of learning in these settings, noting that this often involves collaboration in teams. In these circumstances, the assessment criteria must be determined in each situation. This creates a tension as it highlights the intrinsically local nature of assessment and means that judgements of general achievement based on local practices are not reliable and valid (Knight, 2006). It suggests that helping students to represent their achievements to employers requires differentiated approaches to assessment so that reliable and valid approaches are offered alongside local, contexualised assessment (Knight & Yorke, 2004).

The online environment offers excellent opportunities for contextualised and differentiated approaches to assessment (such as debates, case studies and role plays), while the inclusion of online peer assessment in communities of practice or communities of inquiry provides valuable dimensions to team work, preparing students for peer review in workplace situations as an aspect of local, contextualised assessment of complex levels of achievement. Developments in games, simulations and virtual worlds represent another dimension of contextualised learning experiences where assessment for and of learning merge, with evidence of reliability and validity transparently identified by the extent to which challenges are met. As we noted in Chapter 2, the related merging of real and virtual worlds potentially offers major benefits for assessment in life and work settings where simulated experiences offer immediate evidence of a student's ability in related 'real world' contexts.

Communicating the assessment task

Although this may seem like stating the obvious, it is important to ensure that you communicate your online assessment requirements clearly and completely to students. This includes details of the task itself and how you will grade it, as well as scheduling and submission arrangements. This is particularly important for summative assessment in a fully online teaching environment where your opportunities for ensuring that students understand the requirements are more limited. To avoid misinterpretation by students (or repeated requests for clarification), try to think of all the questions students are likely to ask about a topic and convert your answers to a piece of one-way communication. Be especially careful in setting out details when complex processes are involved (including group work): multiple communication channels may be necessary. At the same time, design your instructions carefully (perhaps by chunking them appropriately) so students do not have to wade through a large volume of information in order to work out what they need to do!

For example ...

Task

You will conduct a debate on a given topic. You will be assigned to a syndicate either on the affirmative or negative side. Details of your syndicate, the topics, resources and guidelines are given on the LMS site for this subject. You will research your topic and use the allocated online discussion space to prepare your arguments, including preparing for:

- the opening statement of your case;
- refuting the opposing argument;
- defending your argument; and
- your closing argument.

The debate will be conducted in class time.

Assessment

The debate activity is a group assignment which contributes up to 15 per cent of your final mark: 5 per cent for preparation and 10 per cent for delivery of the debate.

Your work will be assessed from your discussion posts and the debate itself according to the guidelines for conducting the debate given on the LMS site.

Schedule

- Week 3 (Monday): You will be assigned to a syndicate and given a topic.
- Weeks 3 to 5: Research the topic and discuss online within your syndicate.
- Week 5: Conduct the debate in class.
- Week 6: Grades will be released on the LMS site.

For first year students, detailed information on expectations relating to literacy, content and referencing (and also cheating and plagiarism) is particularly important. Even when your purpose for assessment is diagnostic you need to tell students why you are assessing them, for what (what aspect you are trying to diagnose), and what you will do with the information (if you diagnose a difficulty, will you help students resolve it?). Sometimes the provision of model answers can be a great help to students.

In summative assessment you will need to articulate the criteria by which students will be judged to have been successful in meeting each objective. This is not necessarily a one-to-one relationship; you may have several criteria addressing one objective and/or one criterion which respond to aspects of several objectives. Both the objectives and the assessment criteria should be made clear to students.

For example ...

In the debate example above you may also assess students individually on the basis of a report on the debate itself where they discuss both sides of the argument and arrive at a conclusion. Including objectives and assessment criteria in the instructions ensures that students know what is required of them and how they will be assessed.

Objectives

In successfully completing this activity you will:

1. use research to underpin an argument;
2. identify contentious and controversial issues and discuss from multiple perspectives;
3. synthesise a consensus; and
4. reflect on your development.

Task

After you have debated the topic as a group you will individually write a report of 750 words (± 10%), with the following structure:

- Summarise the debate arguments:
  - opening arguments for each side
  - criticisms of opposing arguments
  - closing arguments for each side.
- Discuss the arguments presented to arrive at a conclusion:
  - synthesis of all arguments, addressing both sides
  - recommendations with resolution of conflict.
- Debrief on the experience of group work:
  - What was your role?
  - What did you like about working in a group?
  - What would you do differently next time?
  - What were the main frustrations?
  - What did you learn?

Submission

The report is due at the end of Week 6. Submit your report as a Word or pdf document in the assignment submission box in the LMS site for the subject with the file name your-last-name_debate_report.doc (or pdf).

Marking guide	Proportion of mark
Report: 750 words (±10%)	80%

- Documentation of debate (150 to 200 words) 30%; accuracy and relevance of information (15%); writing skills (10%); breadth and depth of content (5%).
- Discussion reaching consensus (550 to 600 words) 50%; equal weight to scientific thinking, problem solving and writing skills.

Debrief appended to report (50 to 100 words)

- Equal weight to reflective skills and writing skills.   20%

In this example Objective 1 is addressed in criteria referring to 'accuracy and relevance of information' and 'breadth and depth of content'; and Objectives 2 and 3 are addressed in criteria referring to scientific thinking and problem solving; Objective 4 is addressed in all parts of the task.

This section has illustrated issues related to assessment that are generally applicable. Now we will consider particular uses of the online environment that can benefit assessment.

Using the online environment for assessment

Uses of the online environment that are available for both formative and summative assessment fall into the four main categories indicated in Table 4.2. Each use offers opportunities for reconceptualising assessment to increase authenticity but usually these opportunities will be greater in relation to the last two (online discussion and web publishing).

We will now address each of these uses, discussing issues that they raise and summarising opportunities and challenges that you may need to consider. Bear in mind your learning objectives, your students' characteristics and your learning and teaching context, to identify the points that are relevant to you. The opportunities can be pedagogical, managerial or administrative, and the benefits can be to students, teachers or both. It is helpful to identify the nature of the benefits you expect so you can offset them against challenges.

Table 4.2   Uses of the online environment for assessment

Uses	Examples
1. **Submission** of items for assessment	■ Essays: discursive, descriptive, analytical ■ Reports: CBL, PBL ■ Reviews: critical, analytical ■ Media: image, audio, video, presentation
2. **Automated assessment** ■ quizzes ■ multimedia	■ Multiple choice ■ Short answer ■ Calculation ■ Matching ■ Fill blanks ■ True/false ■ Matching ■ Drag and drop ■ Simulations
3. **Online discussions**	■ Forums: case analysis, project development ■ Debates ■ Allocated roles: lead, summarise, provoke ■ Role plays
4. **Web publishing**	■ E-portfolios ■ Webpages: blogs, wikis ■ Shared documents: Google Documents

Use 1: Submission of items

Assignment submission is the most frequent use of the online environment for assessment (mainly summative assessment). It is the simplest form of online assessment to implement (though the administrative aspect of compiling grades online can be more complex).

Online submission is most likely to be used when an assessment item is a piece of work prepared by an individual student, for example, an essay. It facilitates the management of the assessment process by simplifying submission and return of assignments and keeping a record of this process (including dates and times). You can provide an assignment cover sheet for students to download, complete and submit as the first page of their assignment. The cover sheet may have been developed for paper copy completion so you will need to guide students to complete the declaration by typing their name rather than submitting a signature. Alternatively, you can use the online environment to streamline this process.

For example ...

An alternative format for a declaration about plagiarism and collusion can be an electronic check box. The statement can be offered to students as a quiz question where they have to check the 'I accept' box before the assignment submission link is visible to them.

File formats

The item submitted is commonly a Word document, but can be any electronic file format that the assessor can access. Other file formats increase the possibilities for reconceptualising a task to take advantage of the en-vironment. The file format will depend on the nature of the assessment item: for example, an essay in Word format; graphics in jpg, gif, png or any of the many other possible image formats; an interview as an audio or video file (mp3, wav, aiff, etc); data in spreadsheet format (Excel); an animation as a multimedia file (Flash, exe, etc.); a webpage or website (html); or a presentation might be submitted as a PowerPoint file. In the last case, consider adapting the file format to one which suits the medium. A PowerPoint file, which is designed to support a presentation, even when annotated, may not be the most efficient format in terms of preparation (for the student) and marking (for the assessor). For instance, the same assessment item could be submitted as a Word document or html file. *Choosing the best file format for an assessment item is an important aspect of online assessment design.*

For example ...

For addressing a competency-based objective such as 'demonstrate competence in venous access' students could provide video evidence of their achievement. The video could be annotated via a 'voice-over' explanation of significant issues. Annotation could also be in the form of text incorporated into the video or as a separate document.

Giving students options in regard to the file format may allow them wider choice in the way they express themselves and expand opportunities for creativity. The key point here is that attention to something as simple as a file format can provide an easy way of making an assessment task more authentic. In this case an existing task may be transposed to the online environment, but the way students present their responses is reconceptualised. You will need to consider equivalence in assessing alternate file formats, ensuring that students are able to meet the criteria whatever format they use, and that those who do not have access to some technologies which may enhance presentation are not penalised.

For example ...

In allowing students to create a video instead of writing an essay but not mandating the video format you will need to decide how to equate the video with the essay, ensuring that the criteria you use do not selectively advantage one or other format. Creativity in presentation may be demonstrated using alternative formats but be specific about the nature of the creativity you are assessing; using new technology is not necessarily displaying creativity of ideas. Creativity which indicates new ways of thinking may be expressed in many ways including graphic design, writing, animation, video, etc.

A submitted assignment can be downloaded, assessed and returned electronically to students with comments. Where an assignment is in Word format, feedback to students can be given as 'tracked changes' on the file itself, or in a separate file (for example, Word, Excel). Pdf is a secure format for giving feedback to students. A student submission converted into pdf format can be annotated, have a marking sheet or other file attached, and be returned electronically.

A practical issue to consider in designing the assessment item is the likely size of submitted files. This has implications for the time taken and bandwidth required for students to upload, and implications in terms of class size.

For example ...

An electronic text document is likely to be small in size, but where students include images or graphics in their assignments file sizes can become significant. Large numbers of students trying to submit large files close to a submission deadline may encounter difficulties. Scheduling the submission with a buffer time so students can submit for a period after the cut-off time may alleviate problems.

Successive submissions

Assignment components can be submitted successively, 'building' an assessment item in stages, and progressing from formative to summative assessment. As mentioned previously, assessing in this way can help address plagiarism concerns as progress can be monitored.

For example ...

- Early in a semester students might submit an essay plan on which you can give formative feedback. They could then develop the plan into a final submission, either directly or in stages.
- For an early assessment task, you might also use a submission tool diagnostically. If you wish to know something about the

experience of your students, you could require them to submit an example of previous work or a summary of past experience – or ask them to undertake one of the diagnostic tasks mentioned previously, such as writing a letter about themselves, or commenting on their goals for the unit. This could then be related to subsequent formative and summative items. Of course, if you want everyone to share their experiences then you would use a discussion space.

Table 4.3 summarises some opportunities and challenges relating to online submission of assignments.

Table 4.3 Submission of items for assessment – opportunities and challenges

Examples	Opportunities	Challenges
■ Essays: discursive, descriptive, analytical ■ Reports: case-based learning, problem-based learning ■ Reviews: critical, analytical ■ Media: image, audio, video, presentation	■ Offer management/administrative/advantages ■ Offer flexibility of time, place ■ Accommodate many file types ■ Allow use of plagiarism software ■ Allow sharing of assessment items with other teachers/institutions ■ Support group submission and marking ■ Are faster than mail	■ Have file size limitations ■ May rely on bandwidth ■ Feedback is not immediate ■ Some assessors prefer to print assignments and mark-up the hard copy ■ Require appropriate marking criteria for alternative file types

Use 2: Automated assessment

Assessment items which are automatically delivered to students, then scored and returned to them with automatic feedback, can be effective and efficient for both teachers and learners. This use illustrates interaction with the computer interface as a form of activity that is possible in the online environment which we did not discuss in Chapter 3 because it is usually implemented for formative or summative assessment purposes.

The most commonly used form of automatic assessment is the quiz, but interactive multimedia programs can also offer valuable learning and assessment opportunities. Whatever your use of quizzes, the tracking potential of the online environment can offer valuable insights into your students' learning. This may help you to identify common misunderstandings and misconceptions easily, allowing you to focus student learning more effectively.

Quizzes for formative assessment

In Chapter 2 we discussed the use of an online quiz to provide automated feedback for learning. In the example we used (Figure 2.3) feedback was given for each of the multiple choices offered. Quizzes also provide effective opportunities for self assessment and revision for students. Just as text books often have a quiz at the end of a chapter, an online quiz at the end of a topic can give students a measure of how well they have addressed the chapter or topic. A significant benefit of online quizzes is that feedback is immediate. If feedback is not incorporated into self assessment quizzes, valuable opportunities for learning and motivating are missed. Feedback in quizzes is more complex for short answer and paragraph type questions than for other quiz formats, but model answers can provide points of comparison and can be programmed in advance to give students immediate feedback.

For example ...

Purpose	Feedback
Encouragement*	'Well done'
	'Think about the terms used and try again.'
Explanation*	'That's correct. The... .'
	'Consider the role of the cell membrane in osmosis. Try again.'
Model answer	'Compare your answer with this model answer, prepared by an expert (or former student).'

* As noted previously, feedback is most effective when encouragement and explanation are combined.

Quizzes for summative assessment

If you are using online quizzes for summative assessment you need to consider verification and invigilation as well as technical issues relating to numbers of students concurrently accessing material. Conducting the test in a computer laboratory is the easiest way to provide for security and also technical troubleshooting. However, this removes one of the major advantages of online quizzes – the ability to provide some flexibility in the time and place of testing. Strategies for summative testing which address verification to some extent include:

- scheduling the test to be undertaken within a limited time from commencement (while making it available over a broader timeframe);
- permitting students to see only one question at a time and not allowing each question to be revisited;
- including some short answer questions which relate to other authentic assessment items they have completed; and
- using question banks which are large enough to randomise equivalent questions within different sections of the test.

For example ...

From a bank of questions each student can be allocated a different set of questions randomly generated by an LMS and the risk of cheating in summative assessment is reduced. Random selection of questions from a bank can also have benefits for self assessment and learning as students can complete the quiz repeatedly, gaining further benefit each time.

A significant advantage of using quizzes in the online environment is the potential for students to see high quality images (see Figure 4.2). However, when images are integral to a quiz for summative assessment you must consider the time taken to download them.

Multimedia options

Multiple levels of assessment can be built into interactive multimedia applications which are included in LMS sites. The cost of production may be warranted if the application addresses a learning problem that

Figure 4.2   An image-based quiz question*

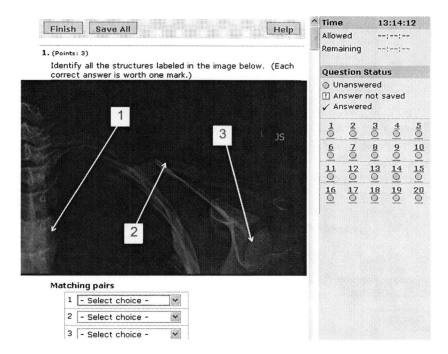

*This image appears online at a high resolution showing detail not evident in the print version.

has been difficult to address in other ways and they offer more flexibility in design than LMS tools.

For example …

■ A molecular mechanism is difficult to describe in words and static pictures do not indicate how molecules interact. In this case an animation of the mechanism can be helpful, and students can be guided to make decisions (for instance, via a drag-and-drop activity) and receive feedback depending on their decision.

■ In Chapter 2 we showed an example of a multimedia version of a multiple choice question (Figure 2.4). This was one question in a large programme of activities that students complete to explore DNA structure. In this particular question students identify the nature of the bonds between DNA strands. The consequences of their decision are 'played out' in animations to explore why they have chosen correctly (or not). Students receive the feedback automatically as soon as they make their selection.

These types of activities provide good opportunities for diagnostic and self assessment, and the automatic aspect makes them useful for formative assessment. They are only optimal for summative assessment if they have a built in scoring and/or auditing facility which allows student tracking and grading.

Table 4.4 summarises some of the opportunities and challenges associated with automated assessment.

Table 4.4 Automated assessment – opportunities and challenges

Examples	Opportunities	Challenges

■ Quizzes:
   – Multiple choice
   – Short answer
   – Matching
   – Calculation
   – Fill blanks
   – True/false
 ■ Multimedia:
   – Drag and drop
   – Matching
   – Simulations
	■ Allow instant feedback
	 ■ Are time effective
	 ■ Support self assessment
	 ■ Support diagnostic assessment
	 ■ Allow accuracy of marking
	 ■ Allow consistency across sites
	 ■ Checking progress is easy
	 ■ Provide for use of high quality images
	 ■ Are low maintenance
	 ■ Are easily updated and improved (LMS tool)
		■ Require measures to ensure authentication (verification) when used summatively
		 ■ Offer only limited feedback on paragraph questions, without opportunities for clarification
		 ■ Restrict creativity
		 ■ Assess only skills and knowledge that can be computer marked
		 ■ Require consideration of logistical issues: hardware, software, bandwidth
		 ■ Multimedia options are time consuming to design, require technical knowledge to develop, and may be costly

Use 3: Online discussions

The options that we have considered for online assessment so far have addressed assessment of items and feedback to individuals. Now we will look at online opportunities for communication and collaboration that can involve individual, peer or group assessment. Online discussions are easily and quickly set up and provide excellent opportunities for formative and summative assessment.

Formative assessment

A major benefit of the use of online discussions for formative assessment is that they allow prompt feedback to students on common queries and difficulties, or on set activities. An administrative advantage to you is that you only have to provide the feedback once. Peer assessment often occurs when students respond to queries from others. You can encourage this generally (through positive reinforcement) or more specifically by asking individual students to respond to a query or issue.

Summative assessment

When learning objectives include verbal communication, collaboration or project management, summative assessment via online discussion is a good option. In defining your expectations consider the design of the assessed online discussion task, as well as how you will grade the discussion.

- **Designing an assessed discussion task:** Discussions may be used to help students complete a task individually or as part of a group. The discussion itself may represent the assessment item or the discussion may contribute to the development of an assessment item.

For example ...

A discussion of a particular topic or question (such as a debate) may form the assessed item, or you may want to see evidence of collaboration in producing a project report (or other project output). If the discussion is the assessment item then the assessment criteria will identify the answers to the following questions.

You will need to consider questions such as: Will student participation be enough or will you assess the content of students' posts? How many posts will students need to make? Will the quality of their writing matter? Will they need to cover particular content? Will students need to respond to each other or just post for all to read? Will peer commentary be important? If students need to engage with each other, will they do that on a one-to-one basis or on a one-to-many basis?

For example ...

Will you require students to comment on a post by one other student, or to synthesise a new argument or idea out of posts of several (or all) of the other students? Will you have a presence in the discussion?

If an objective of assessing a discussion is related to students' project management skills then it might be important to stay out of the discussion. If you are assessing the content of their posts and students are straying off the track, then your contribution to put the discussion back on track may be invaluable for learning as well as for the assessment. By giving formative feedback during the discussion you can assure students that they are addressing the objectives appropriately.

As for all assessment items, students need to know the timeframe of the discussion. For students in early years of their studies and those unfamiliar with online discussions, specifying a timeline for each post as well the final post or due date can help relieve their anxiety. As we mentioned in Chapter 3, it is often important to provide specific dates: one for when an initial posting is required; and another for commentary on initial postings. Otherwise, students posting late contributions can place unfair pressure on other students by not allowing them sufficient time to make a required response.

Where a discussion is used for assessment early in the semester, students often need to be given considerable support to ensure that they have solved access and technical issues and are comfortable with the online environment. You should avoid setting complex discussion tasks too early. Use of Salmon's (2003) model for teaching and learning online can help you to develop tasks of increasing complexity to meet higher level learning objectives as the semester progresses.

> **For example ...**
>
> - At the information exchange stage of Salmon's model (Stage 3) you might ask students to search for evidence about the social impact of natural disasters and make a brief posting providing a resource they found and explaining why they selected it.
> - Later, at Stage 5, you might ask them to analyse the resources provided by the class (perhaps, along with other information that you provide), to prepare a final piece of work on this topic that includes recommendations for action at some level.

Although innovative assessable activities involve reconceptualisation, you can also simply transpose activities that you might run in a classroom to the online mode with the advantage that a record of discussion and the inputs of individuals is created. Further advantages for students include flexibility in relation to time and place, and the ability to take time to research topics and craft posts. This can be a particular advantage for shy students and those for whom English is a second language. As explained in Chapter 3, you also have the option of scheduling students as e-moderators. Their performance of this role could be part of your assessment of them (if it relates to the objectives) or it could be a valuable opportunity for them to undertake the role of assessor.

- **Scoring contributions to discussion:** The mark allocated to a discussion as a proportion of the overall mark for the unit should be consistent with the objectives that the discussion addresses. Your answers to the questions we asked about designing an assessed discussion task will have an impact on scoring.

> **For example ...**
>
> - You may allocate a small number of marks for participation in a discussion regardless of the content if the purpose is to form a community.
> - The content of discussion posts could be allocated marks when students are asked to critique a piece of work (an article, another student's work, etc.).

> Marks for the quality of writing might be relevant where objectives include writing skills, or where discussion contributions form part of a larger assessment item.

You need to consider how you will differentiate and award group and individual marks. In considering your expectations of students you are defining criteria for assessment.

- **Assessing group work via discussions:** Online discussions provide an excellent avenue for assessing group work because of the record of individual contributions. This helps address the issue of student dissatisfaction with group work mentioned earlier. Student negotiations around working as a team can be used as evidence of collaborative skills, and contributions of content and ideas can be attributed to individuals. The discussion may be the sole output for assessment or may be used to assess collaborative and individual components where the output, which is also assessed, is external to the discussion. The external item might be a document such as a report, a website, a video or audio, a presentation or even a performance.

For example ...

Debates

The competitive nature of a debate lends itself to assessment. Engagement in tension and conflict is a powerful motivator at many levels.

Assessable online debates need to be structured and scheduled carefully and are often best left until later in the semester to allow students to become familiar with the online environment and the assessment requirements. Conducting a preliminary online debate which is formatively assessed can be useful in giving students practice and giving you a sense of the issues of engagement for your students. If this aspect of group work is part of the objectives of the debate then the preliminary debate provides a good opportunity and motivation for the students to engage so they are prepared for the summative assessment. In addition to grading of the group achievement, the contributions of each member of the group can be assessed and individuals can be graded. You may record two grades, a group mark and an individual mark, or you may scale the group mark by a factor depending on the level of contribution of the individual.

Ensure that criteria for these types of group work objectives are included for summative assessment.

Case studies

Online discussions are frequently used to analyse a particular case, or to compare cases. Typically, the case is presented through a scenario and this triggers group discussion. A case may be presented as a single scenario or unfold as discussion progresses, as noted earlier. Refer back to Figure 2.1 for an example. The output of the analysis, whether it is a summary of the discussion or a more formal report, is an obvious item for assessment but the discussion itself may provide rich evidence of students meeting objectives.

Role plays

When using online role play in assessment you need to ensure that it has an appropriate resolution which satisfies students and justifies their involvement, in addition to the marks they are awarded. It should be followed with a debriefing phase. Grades will probably need to be determined through carefully designed assessment criteria specified in an assessment rubric. This type of activity is excellent for involving students in identifying the assessment criteria.

Table 4.5 summarises some of the main opportunities and challenges associated with assessing online discussions.

Use 4: Web publishing

Benefits of web publishing for assessment include the potential for authenticity and the motivational value of preparing work to be published which then contributes to improving the quality of the learning outcomes.

Table 4.5   Online discussion for assessment – opportunities and challenges

Examples	Opportunities	Challenges
■ Allocated roles: lead, summarise, provoke ■ Debates ■ Forums: case analysis, project development ■ Role plays	■ Are flexible in terms of time and place ■ Are easy to set up ■ Allow feedback by teachers/participants ■ Allow all to see diverse opinions/interpretations ■ Keep a record of work ■ Facilitate peer assessment ■ Support reflective responses ■ Support shy participants	■ Can be time consuming to give feedback ■ May require careful planning and management (e.g., role plays) ■ Can be difficult to assess summatively ■ Allow some participants to 'hide' ■ Limit spontaneity ■ Lack social cues

A published outcome may also highlight the benefits of working in groups on collaborative projects. The opportunity to compare and critique the published work provides further avenues for extending the quality of the learning outcomes. We use the term 'web publishing' to include contexts where the outcome is available to the world (open access on the internet), or a subset of viewers which may range from a large number (e.g., everyone in your institution) to just two people, the student and yourself. Depending on the nature of the task, you may need to provide students with guidance on writing for the web, including writing style, usability (including linking) and visual layout. Informal writing may be suitable for a personal journal or microblogging, whereas a webpage may require a specific style and format.

For example ...

If students are preparing a webpage or site for marketing a product then presentation will be an important assessment criterion.

In this section we cover again common ways in which students might create and publish content on the web that we looked at in Chapter 3, in order to make some comments on the use for assessment of:

- e-portfolios
- blogs
- wikis
- shared documents, and
- student podcasting.

We do not list mobile technologies separately in this section because their use can contribute to all of the above, in capturing data that is used in published content, or in its dissemination. Dissemination could involve open publication on the internet (e.g. videos uploaded to YouTube). Data captured by mobile technologies may also be included in the submission of items for assessment and could be related to discussion items that are assessed (Uses 1 and 3).

E-portfolios

If you are using e-portfolios in your learning design you will be able to configure the software to streamline assessment. Students will be able to collect relevant evidence required for assessment and integrate the feedback they receive. It is important that the control of the e-portfolio 'publishing' remains in the hands of the student to derive maximum benefit from both learning processes and the products to be published. The student will prepare the 'published' view by selecting the required evidence and annotating it appropriately.

For example ...

As evidence of project planning you may have asked students to submit a concept map with a reflective commentary (annotation) on how they approached the mapping exercise.

Blogs

To facilitate students' reflective practice you may have chosen to use blogs. Like an e-portfolio, this is predominantly an individual activity but one in which the technology allows for immediate and targeted feedback to the author (student) by others. In terms of assessment, a key aspect of a blog is its chronological nature which provides evidence of development over time.

> ## For example ...
>
> Students could submit a link to the blog they kept while on a practical placement, or for logging a process of work during a project.

This is suited to a continuous assessment strategy. While you may restrict access to the blog if it is an assessment item, in some cases (depending on your objectives) an open blog will contribute to its authenticity and you might include consideration of appropriate comments by members of the public in assessing the extent to which the blog meets its purpose.

Similarly, while you may think microblogging an unlikely option for assessment, it could provide useful evidence of the ability to present key ideas briefly, with responses by members of the public validating the extent to which it meets its purpose.

Wikis

In contrast to e-portfolios and blogs, wikis are suited to co-creation of content by groups of users and to assessment of group processes and products. In Figure 2.6 we showed the homepage of the output of one student group in a project which was undertaken using a wiki. As we have mentioned, a significant problem in assessing group work has been student dissatisfaction when contributions of group members are uneven. The visibility of all contributions and the process of the group work recorded in the history of a wiki effectively address this aspect of assessing group work.

> ## For example ...
>
> All contributions to a wiki page can be viewed via the page history and this gives a record of all changes whether or not they end up in the published view. Along with the discussions occurring in the wiki, the process of the group work is recorded.

Shared documents

If a group assessment task is to create a Word document, web-based applications such as Google Documents may be a good option. Students work on preparing the file and can export it for submission or inclusion in a larger project.

> **For example ...**
>
> Your group project might involve students in investigating a topic or case study. You might have added authenticity to it by asking them to prepare a report for a professional body. They will need to submit it to the professional body as an appropriately structured and formatted document. This can be done online with a web-based word processor.

Student podcasting

If students have engaged in podcasting as a learning activity you may simply assess the audio or video product of the activity. A reason for choosing podcasting as an activity may have been ease of access for students and this will be a benefit for you as an assessor also. However, you could also consider the skills that students would have developed in the process of creating the podcast, including technical aspects as well as those related to syndication, such as choosing appropriate metadata.

> **For example ...**
>
> Set up a site where students upload their audio or video files. Students turn the media file into a podcast by including metadata such as a title, author, date, subject keywords. They could extend the reach of the podcast by creating connections (via feeds) to other related sites. This context for their media file could be part of the assessment.

Table 4.6 summarises some of the opportunities and challenges associated with the use of web publishing for assessment.

Supporting students

We stated at the beginning of the chapter that our assumption was that online assessment should either offer a benefit to student learning or, at least, should not inhibit it. We also suggested that considering your learners' characteristics and the context of their learning was an important

Table 4.6	Web publishing for assessment: opportunities and challenges	
Examples	**Opportunities**	**Challenges**
■ E-portfolios ■ Webpages: blogs, wikis ■ Shared documents: Google Documents ■ Student podcasts	■ Support reflective practice/self assessment ■ Support group work ■ Facilitate peer learning and feedback ■ Facilitate interactivity ■ Encourage authentic practice ■ Improve web publishing skills	■ Require development of web publishing skills ■ Lack social cues ■ Can be time intensive ■ Require validation of content (potential for plagiarism)

aspect of assessment design. In addition to the specific knowledge that you have about your students, you should check that you have addressed the following general issues.

■ Have you considered student support when you designed your assessment tasks, particularly if the technology or the assessment approaches are new to them? Have you established technical support procedures *and conveyed them clearly* to your students?

■ In considering the above questions, have you allowed for diversity among your students, including issues such as access and equity, variations in competence with the technology, the needs of international students, and any costs or ethical issues?

■ Have you discussed with students their responsibilities and your expectations of them, relating to issues such as: participation; self, peer or group assessment; authentication; and specific arrangements relating to online assessment tasks? This requires you to think about the way you communicate with your students and might involve consideration of learning contracts or other approaches to demonstrate student involvement in and commitment to the approaches that are being implemented.

■ Above all, are you approachable and is this evident to your students? Online assessment, particularly when it is not undertaken in a computer laboratory and is used summatively, can result in high levels of anxiety for many students, and given the potential for high transactional distance in these situations, it is extremely important that students know what to do, and that they will receive a sympathetic response and practical assistance, should problems arise.

Your ability to support your students may depend to a large extent on your ability to support yourself and to manage the situation. This ranges from managing broad technical, security and integrity issues to personal issues relating to your own use of the online environment for assessment, and managing the particular characteristics of your students. In the following section we will consider some of the broad issues relating to management of the environment first and then move to some of the specific management and administrative skills you may need to have.

Managing and administering assessment

Technical aspects

You would not be considering online assessment unless you were sure that both you and your students had access to appropriate hardware and software, and also appropriate bandwidth if students will be accessing their assessment tasks outside the university. It is worthwhile conducting an audit to check your students' levels of access before you proceed with your planning, particularly if you are considering the use of timed summative assessment tasks. While you may be reasonably sure of the security of an LMS platform, there is always the possibility of technical problems when technology is used so you should have a backup plan in case of problems.

Some specific issues to consider include the following.

- Ensure that your students can authenticate their access to the online environment in which you are offering assessment, and that they know where they can receive support on such issues.

- Will students need to download large files as part of their assessment? This is especially important for tasks conducted within limited timeframes.

For example ...

You will need to make special arrangements for any students who are likely to be disadvantaged by their access to the technology. Where a student has a dial-up modem or limited access to a computer (such as in a library), make arrangements for them to have additional time, or for them to have upgraded access for the assessment period (such as in a computer laboratory on campus).

- Have you taken into account scheduled platform maintenance periods? If you are planning a major online assessment activity where timing is critical, contact your platform administrator to help you to maximise the possibility that no unscheduled disruptions affect your assessment.

- If you are using a system that is not institutionally supported (for example, blogs or wikis that contain assessable work), then it is *extremely important* that you take responsibility for investigating access and security issues and arranging backup procedures with and for your students.

When things go wrong there is often a tendency by students (and staff!) to 'blame the technology'. A cautious approach to technical issues will prevent many potential problems from occurring but, as indicated above, you should always have a backup plan. The second part of this equation is to make sure that students know what to do if technical problems arise. Make sure you make the most of the technical support available within your institution. If there is a helpdesk make sure you know how to access it, when it is active and the type of support it offers. Direct your students to this support rather than trying to solve technical problems yourself. Your time is better spent supporting them in their learning.

Authentication

Authentication issues are often at the heart of staff reservations about the use of online assessment: 'How will I know whether the student or someone else completed the task?' Of course, the same question can be asked about almost all assignments that students submit which are not written in an examination room. This issue can be addressed, in part, through attention to assessment design. We have already mentioned design strategies which help to address authentication concerns but we summarise some of them again below.

- It will be more difficult for someone else to impersonate the student if the assessment items occur in a tightly structured sequence, where each successive component builds upon the previous one and/or where these require analysis of the student's own inquiry and experience, possibly related to the development of portfolios of work. Authentic assessment items, by their nature, tend to work against plagiarism.

- The online environment is extremely beneficial in keeping a record of the process in the development of an assignment, as well as providing a variety of ways for presenting the final product. Assessment tasks where you can see development taking place in the online environment, or those that include commentary on products as they develop, provide useful ways of monitoring authentication.

- Randomisation of questions and careful timing helps to limit collusion between students when quizzes are used, with completion in computer laboratories an option for on-campus students.

The issues of cheating and plagiarism are of huge concern, irrespective of whether assessment is conducted online, although, of course, it is access to the internet that has expanded the ease with which students can obtain and misuse information. You should be familiar with your institution's definitions relating to cheating, plagiarism and collusion. We noted earlier the inclusion of assignment cover sheets with assessment submissions or an equivalent online declaration. These allow you to meet institutional requirements regarding use and inclusion of plagiarism information for non-examination assessment.

It is important that students can identify plagiarism and issues of attribution, so provide information and links to resources within your institution or beyond. Alternatively, you may go further and design an activity which involves identification of plagiarism in content related to subject matter that your students are studying.

For example ...

If your institution uses plagiarism software, an activity which you can include where text submission is part of assessment, is to require students to subject their assignment to the software prior to submission and submit the report with their assignment.

This has potential for richer learning outcomes. While the use of plagiarism software can be viewed as a deterrent, it is also a learning opportunity for students who are not always aware of the nature of plagiarism. Keep in mind the limitations of the software and ensure you discuss its implications with students. This again relates to student support, helping them (especially new students) to understand what is expected of them so that penalties are clearly a matter of last resort.

Your administrative skills

While online assessment offers a number of administrative benefits, your ability to access these will depend on developing your own skills in relation to the tasks involved. Below we cover some of the tasks you may need to undertake.

Setting up your site

Administrative tasks involved in setting up your site for assessment include organising the assessment tools required for assignment submission, discussions, creating quizzes or web publishing. If you are using any aspects of group assessment you will need to be able to divide students into groups. If discussion topics are used for individual or group activity, you might also want to think about naming conventions for messages relating to specific assessment components, as well as providing information about netiquette and advice relating to the length, timing and other requirements for specific postings. There may also be a range of additional tools or resources that you need to add to the site, depending on the nature of the assessment.

Managing grades

If you are using an LMS, you are likely to have access to an administrative tool for managing grades. This is a spreadsheet within the system for storing student records. Grades are automatically created for automated assessment tasks with pre-determined answers, such as multiple choice tests. Assignments that you manually grade within the system can also be automatically added to the appropriate column. You can hide or reorder columns, and include columns for assessment that are undertaken outside the system. You can include both alphabetical and numerical information and can release grades to students via the tool available for this. You can create columns to calculate end of semester/term grades and you can download the file to your computer and open this as a spreadsheet. Once you are able to manage this efficiently it should save you a lot of time in managing assessment and provide a concurrent benefit to students by speeding up their receipt of feedback.

Managing workload

A major concern that is frequently raised by teaching staff about teaching or assessing online is the workload involved. In relation to assessment, particular concerns emerge if you are implementing continuous assessment through related activities, or assessing online discussion which requires ongoing e-moderation. Once again, we would urge you to consider carefully your assessment design, in conjunction with the question of 'who assesses?' in order to identify strategies that are manageable while also contributing to the quality of learning.

Managing risks

Having considered the uses of the online environment for assessment and some of the opportunities and challenges, together with a range of support, management and administrative issues, you will now be in a good position to evaluate the risks associated with implementing online assessment. Table 4.7 provides an example of a simple way of doing this. Rating risk factors as high, medium or low will allow you to assess whether a risk is acceptable or not in your context and what you might do about it.

With rapid evolution of technologies the nature and level of risks change so it is important to review them periodically.

Table 4.7   Risks associated with online assessment

Risk factors	Risk level L, M, H*	Risk details (examples)
Student support		■ Access and equity issues ■ Requires guidance – expectations, logins, troubleshooting
Technical issues		■ Access to appropriate hardware and software ■ Setting up assessment, service interruptions, bandwidth
Authentication/ plagiarism		■ Cheating, collusion and plagiarism
Your administrative skills		■ Requires ability to use software (download, mark and upload items), manage grades, and provide support ■ Workload ■ Copyright

* Low, Medium, High

Illustrating the ideas in this chapter ...

Suzy continues her story below to illustrate how she addressed aspects of online assessment.

Suzy's story continued ...

My experience of designing the digital response assessment task to help students meet objectives relating to integration of theory and practice has meant working backwards from that to design the activities, resources and supports that they would need. This has had a huge impact on my thinking about the nature and purposes of assessment.

I began to see that the online learning environment offered me the means of framing the relationship between theory and practice so that the assessment could authentically drive the learning and teaching process. By using the online learning environment to draft their first philosophy statement, the context which the pre-service teachers created for this statement became real: theory became immediately relevant to them because it was embedded in practice via that statement. Evidence that students were aware of this relationship was demonstrated in their reflections later in the semester. For example :

...instead of regurgitating the information we received through lectures and readings, this task required us to provide a context for the information instead. This meant we really had to think about the information we had and how it could be used within our practice.

I was impressed by the above statement because the reference to use of information 'within our practice' showed a leap forward from 'applying theory to practice' and I saw in this the gains that could be made by 'teaching through assessment'. Although I already knew about the concepts of authentic assessment, formative assessment ('assessment for learning') and summative assessment ('assessment of learning'), I felt that I had moved beyond these ideas. I saw a fundamental link between online learning and teaching through assessment as the pre-service teachers created and 'published' their own assessable content which demonstrated the theory/practice relationship.

Although 'assessment for learning' was close to what I was doing, it did not have the same link with online learning and it did not unify the concepts of learning, teaching and assessment in the same way. The process by which the content was created was visible to all participants (including me). The pre-service teachers themselves played a peer assessment role, and formative and summative assessment, communication and scheduling of assessment tasks, constructive alignment, authenticity, and dealing with plagiarism were all embedded in the process, encompassing support of students and management of the environment as well.

Thus, online learning removed the need for me to lecture which resulted in a dichotomy between theory and practice, and instead provided a context in which the relationship between theory and practice was modelled and discussed. The unity of theory and practice was paralleled by the unification of learning, teaching and assessment through the processes and outcomes afforded by the online environment.

The use of online discussion and web publishing to create the digital responses could easily be extended to a Web 2.0 environment since the visibility of the group process in the creation of a product is similar to what Web 2.0 technologies offer. This experience has demonstrated to me the highly engaging benefits, for students and myself, of using the online environment to reconceptualise assessment.

Summary

You should now have clearly in mind the relationship between assessment and student learning in order to consider this in designing assessment for the online environment. In identifying reasons for assessing your students, we have distinguished formative and summative assessment and particularly noted the role of formative assessment in enhancing learning. This role has been evident among the assessment design principles we have considered, as has the role of authentic assessment. In preparing for online assessment we have also thought about the potential of self, peer and group assessment and recognised that online assessment may have learning benefits or administrative benefits (or both). We hope that considering assessment in the online environment has helped you to recognise ways to address a wider range or learning outcomes. You should now have a good framework for considering in more detail the way you might use the online environment for assessment, and some of the potential opportunities and challenges.

We continue building the checklist by adding issues related to assessment online. As we mentioned in previous chapters you should feel confident of your grasp of the issues if you can answer 'Yes' to a majority of the items in the list. If that is not the case then you may need to look to colleagues who have been engaged with assessing online and learn from their stories.

Are you able to identify ...	Yes	Unsure	No
23. Your view of the nature and purposes of assessment which will guide you in your online assessment design?			
24. Your answer to the question of 'Who assesses?' and how you might implement this online?			
25. Some principles that will guide you in your online assessment design?			
26. The uses that you will make of the online environment for assessment?			
27. Some of the opportunities and challenges associated with the uses of the online environment you have chosen?			

Are you able to identify ...	Yes	Unsure	No
28. The student support issues relating to online assessment which you may need to consider?			
29. The management and administrative issues relating to online assessment which you may need to consider (and which you could summarise in a risk analysis)?			
30. Any other factors that you may need to consider in designing your online assessment? (Specify below.)			

5

Evaluation

Introduction

Although we have made only passing reference to evaluation so far, in fact, evaluation should permeate the whole process of analysis, design, development and teaching to support online learning and assessment. In this chapter we will introduce some concepts and strategies to help you to do this in simple ways that are not too demanding in terms of the resources you will need, including your time.

We begin by introducing a few evaluation concepts, including some older ideas from the educational evaluation literature, and some more recent ones that relate directly to evaluation of the use of educational technology. We emphasise the value of a cyclical approach which provides an overarching framework that can encompass all of the other evaluation concepts and methods that you choose to use. A cyclical approach also supports the idea that online design, development and implementation is an incremental, iterative process that will involve you in continual refinement of your teaching practice as you draw on the evidence available to you through experience and evaluation. Two other important concepts in this context are the importance of reflection, as part of this cycle, and also the value of taking a pragmatic approach to evaluation. We will expand on these ideas in the next section.

After we have considered these concepts, we will focus specifically on online learning design, development and implementation, suggesting some evaluation methods that you could implement at each of these stages. With these ideas in mind, we will then highlight components that you might consider in designing your evaluation plan, taking into account the purpose and audience of your evaluation. This will include appropriate learner-centred evaluation methods if your purpose is associated with the improvement of student learning. After this we suggest some issues that you might need to address in managing, implementing, reporting and acting on the results of your evaluation.

Once you have established an approach to evaluation that works for you, you should have in place a simple, practical, cyclical framework which draws on the idea of reflective practice to guide you in the iterative improvement of your online teaching and assessment practices.

Some evaluation concepts

The educational evaluation literature has developed rapidly over recent decades, introducing many new concepts that are useful in guiding evaluation. We will only be covering a few of them here, with a particular emphasis on evaluation of educational technology. Underpinning these newer concepts is the seminal work of Scriven (1967) who conceptualised evaluation as a form of inquiry undertaken primarily to determine the worth of something, and of Stufflebeam (1972) who conceptualised evaluation as an aid to decision-making. These two concepts will probably inform any evaluation you undertake to improve your online teaching or assessment practices. Scriven (1967) was also responsible for identifying the concepts of formative and summative evaluation:

> When the cook tastes the soup, it is formative evaluation;
> when the dinner guest tastes the soup, it is summative evaluation.
> (Harvey, 1998, p. 7)

When you are developing online teaching or assessment components, formative evaluation is critical: the time, effort and possibly the cost involved mean that it is vital that you build in formative evaluation at various points to ensure that the emerging online learning environment will allow students to meet the learning objectives successfully.

Another 'old' but useful idea is that of evaluation as illumination (Parlett & Hamilton, 1977). Referring to evaluation in a classroom context, they explained the approach as follows:

> It aims to be both adaptable and eclectic. The choice of research tactics follows not from research doctrine, but from decisions in each case as to the best available techniques: the problem defines the methods used, not *vice versa*. (Parlett & Hamilton, 1977, p. 13)

This idea has been used effectively over recent years by the United States Teaching, Learning and Technology (TLT) Group in its Flashlight Program, conveying the idea of shining a light on whatever it is that needs to be evaluated. The latest version of Flashlight Online uses a Web 2.0 tool (The TLT Group, 2009). With its emphasis on eclecticism and pragmatism, it also closely resembles the concept recommended by Reeves and Hedberg (2003) who suggest using an 'Eclectic-Mixed Methods-Pragmatic Paradigm' when evaluating educational technology as this approach is most capable of handling the complexities of society and technology. At a narrower level, an eclectic and pragmatic approach acknowledges the need for adaptability to support the specific decisions that need to be made in specific contexts which are characteristic of educational evaluation.

As we noted earlier, it is also useful to consider evaluation as part of an ongoing cycle. This is often used as a quality-control approach involving:

- planning
- acting
- evaluating, and
- improving.

Student evaluations of teaching effectiveness frequently use this kind of approach for quality assurance purposes. They are increasingly being used in higher education institutions around the world, often in conjunction with major government initiatives to enhance institutional accountability for benchmarking purposes (Marsh, 2007). Although not usually focused on evaluation of online learning, you could include evaluation data of this kind in the design of your evaluation plan which we will discuss later.

A cyclical approach also fits well with conceptualising the design, development and implementation of online learning and assessment approaches as an iterative process when you are designing your own evaluation strategies. In this way, evaluation can be seen in the context of an *action research* cycle (Figure 5.1). Kember (2000, p. 20) refers to seven features of action research which make it appropriate for quality enhancement in education. It is:

- concerned with social practice;
- aimed towards improvement;
- a cyclical process;
- pursued by systematic inquiry;
- a reflective process;
- participative;
- determined by the practitioners.

Figure 5.1 The action research cycle

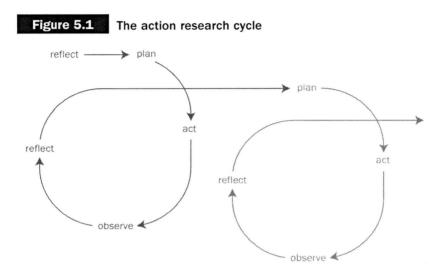

The 'reflect' part of the cycle indicated in Figure 5.1 is particularly important because it allows you and others involved to process the results gained from various evaluation strategies and determine what improvements you will make. A similar approach to evaluation, developed separately from the concept of action research, involves the ideas of reflection-in-action and reflection-on-action (Schön, 1983; 1987) which are often used for evaluation in relation to professional education because they allow for the 'messiness' of the real world. Again, this suggests a pragmatic approach that lends itself well to evaluation during preparation and implementation of online learning and assessment.

Evaluation and online learning design, development and implementation

During the 1990s there were some useful contributions to developing an integrated approach to evaluation for educational technology projects, using a staged approach through design, development, implementation and institutionalisation (Alexander & Hedberg, 1994; Bain, 1999). A third framework, derived from these, was subsequently used by Phillips, Bain, McNaught, Rice and Tripp (2000) in an Australian national project on learning-centred evaluation of computer-facilitated learning projects in higher education. In Table 5.1 we have adapted some elements of these

Table 5.1 An integrated evaluation framework

Purpose	Evaluation questions (examples)	Methods (examples)
Analysis and Design phase		
To provide information for planning	What areas of curriculum where students experience difficulty could be addressed by an online teaching or assessment approach?	■ Interviews with experienced teachers ■ Review of literature on teaching in the subject ■ Review of student achievement in assessment task
	What teaching/ learning/assessment approach is likely to bring about the desired learning outcome?	■ Review of learners, learning context ■ Evaluation of other non technology-based learning strategies (e.g., reflective journals) ■ Review of literature to identify online learning approaches used to bring about this learning outcome
To inform decisions made in the design of the technology-based learning programme	What educational strategy should be used?	■ Review of literature to determine what is known about the way students learn the particular topic
	Are the selected online learning components appropriate for allowing students to achieve the desired learning process and outcomes?	■ Prototyping or storyboarding with potential users and media experts ■ Peer review
Development phase		
To inform decisions made in the development of the technology-based learning programme	Is the user interaction effective and efficient?	■ Observation ■ Videorecording ■ User-tracking ■ Interviews with/of users and expert reviewers

(Continued)

Table 5.1 An integrated evaluation framework (*cont'd*)

Purpose	Evaluation questions (examples)	Methods (examples)
	What and how are students learning (using this programme)?	■ Stimulated recall ■ Critical incidents ■ Think aloud as target students use programme
	What is the merit of this programme?	■ Peer review
Implementation phase		
To determine the worth of the technology-based learning programme in the context of its use	How are students using the online learning environment?	■ User tracking
	What changes in understanding have students undergone as a result of using the online approach in this context?	■ Pre- and post-tests ■ Student questionnaires ■ Student interviews ■ Student focus groups
	Is the online approach a 'valid' way of addressing the stated learning need?	■ Expert/peer review

Source: Adapted from Alexander & Hedberg, 1994; Bain, 1999; Phillips et al., 2000.

frameworks to provide you with examples of the purpose of evaluation during design, development and implementation, the kinds of evaluation questions you might ask, and the methods you might use for answering them at each stage.

Please note:

■ The examples just provide a small sample of the kinds of methods you might use.

■ The nature of the question you ask will often (but not necessarily) determine the nature of the method that lends itself to answering the question.

- We have excluded the 'institutionalisation' phase which refers to transfer of the learning environment beyond the immediate context of the innovation, since we have presumed that your focus is likely to be on the immediate context only.

- Formative evaluation occurs during analysis, design and development and summative evaluation occurs at the implementation phase (though you might also implement formative evaluation processes while implementation is in progress).

Deciding on the evaluation methods you will use

When you use a pragmatic, mixed-methods approach to evaluation, your decisions about the methods will usually be determined by the purpose of the evaluation, the questions you want answered, and a range of practical issues, including resourcing, as your approach to data collection carries implications for time and, potentially, money. Ideally, a mix of quantitative and qualitative evaluation strategies is best since studying an issue using several different methods which allows *triangulation*, will strengthen the validity of the conclusions you draw. Considering the kind of data that you require, and the implications for interpretation, will help you to make decisions about qualitative versus quantitative methods, subject to the availability of resources.

For example ...

If during the development phase you want to know if there are sufficient and appropriate academic resources and support for students to complete an activity you have designed, you may ask a colleague to comment on this issue, thus giving you qualitative data.

At the implementation stage you may want to evaluate the perspectives of your learners on the same issue. In this case you may ask them to rate resources and support generally or particular resources or supports individually. In the former situation you could ask students to rate from 1 to 5 (strongly agree to strongly disagree) the statement that 'the resources provided were sufficient for me to be able to successfully complete the activity', and in the latter, 'Reading x.x on …. provided sufficient information for me to do the … part of the activity.' You could also ask them to comment on the usefulness of a resource, or ask them what other resources they used or needed. This would give you a combination of quantitative and qualitative data.

Because we are focusing on a pragmatic approach to evaluation that is simple for you to implement, we do not suggest that you need to triangulate at every phase, but only when the purpose of the evaluation demands it. In fact, there are many circumstances where you should not underestimate the value of informal feedback – such as passing a draft to an appropriate colleague and asking for comments, or asking students for informal comments during implementation (and also noting unsolicited feedback). You might also include the results of university evaluations of teaching or subjects, which involves no effort on your part in terms of conducting the evaluation (though they will not give you information you might require during design and development). Another reason that triangulation is not always necessary is that if you are also using a cyclical evaluation approach, rigour is achieved through responsiveness to practice (Schön, 1995) so the process of iteration provides an inbuilt quality control mechanism, as we discussed earlier.

Methods mentioned in Table 5.1 include reviews, interviews, observation, questionnaires, tracking, focus groups and pre/post testing. Reviewing what is already known from the literature and what you know about your students and their learning context is important. You might gain this information from documentation and from talking to colleagues (peers) in your own discipline and in education and technology fields. Once you have some ideas 'down on paper' you will want to ask peers and experts to review your plans and give you feedback. This may be through a range of methods including conversation (from informal 'tea-room chat' to formal interview), document mark-up, or written comments and is most likely to be qualitative rather than quantitative. The documentation for evaluation may include text, a concept map, a site map or a storyboard. A storyboard is useful if you are planning a complex site where you are working with others on the development. Keep in mind the skills of those from whom you are seeking feedback: remember that an IT expert will be able to comment on the technology but may not have any perspective on the educational design.

By the time you are into the development stage you are likely to have a prototype of your online environment, or part of it, to try out. Here you will branch out and ask some new people for evaluation feedback, and ask about usability as well as design. You will probably first want to know where the key problems are rather than detailed feedback. When you have addressed these problems and you have developed enough of the prototype for a user to be able to complete a unit of work (such as an activity or an assessment task) you may benefit from observing how users go about studying in the environment, which link they go to first, and so on. Combining this approach with an interview or a focus group can give you valuable data from which you can further develop your prototype. When you think you have developed the prototype sufficiently to be usable by students it is wise to ask 'student-like' users to trial the environment. Students who have just completed the unit for which you are designing the environment, or postgraduate students, are good choices as they are familiar with the subject and will be able to tell you about gaps and inconsistencies.

At this stage you have a beta version of your environment and you are ready to implement it with your first group of students. This is where you will want to make the most of data collected automatically (e.g., user tracking) and choose methods which will allow you to gather data from a relatively larger number of users, such as questionnaires. Videorecording students in a computer laboratory while they use the environment can be useful for observation.

In Table 5.2 we summarise some advantages and issues to consider in relation to common evaluation methods that you might use.

During implementation, if you have access to a learning management system, you can consider the following options for collecting evaluation data.

- Reporting and tracking tools allow you to collect statistics on student activity so you can monitor when, how frequently and for how long students have engaged in or accessed particular parts of the site. This information should be interpreted cautiously: a long time spent on one page may indicate interest, difficulty or a coffee break.

- You can use the online survey tool to evaluate your students' responses to aspects of your online environment. This allows you to use the same

Table 5.2   Comparing some common evaluation methods

Methods	Advantages	Issues to consider
Review of existing documentation/ evidence	■ The evidence already exists; you don't need to design and implement methods for data collection	■ May be time-consuming to search for the information you need, and to analyse and draw conclusions from it
User tracking	■ Simple to implement when tracking is provided by the system you use; may include audit trails, keystroke recordings, and evidence of time spent on particular components, or the number of times they have been accessed	■ May be difficult to interpret: see previous comment about interpreting information from reporting and tracking tools in a learning management system
User logs	■ A valuable method for gaining responses from users as they work through a specific part of your learning environment	■ Requires clear communication of purpose to users (constructing a simple form for them to complete is helpful) ■ Requires users have the time available to complete the task ■ Depending on the way you collect the data, interpretation may be time-consuming
Observation	■ Useful during development for identifying how users handle an online component	■ Interpretation is required; can be combined with a 'think-aloud' approach but this may distort natural usage
Expert/peer review	■ Simple to implement ■ Potential to elicit valuable information	■ Assumes availability of appropriate expert/peer reviewers ■ Requires clear communication of the kind of information you are seeking

Methods	Advantages	Issues to consider
Interview	<ul><li>Simple to design</li><li>Simple to implement</li><li>Potential to elicit rich qualitative data</li></ul>	<ul><li>Time-consuming if a number of interviews are undertaken</li><li>Requires recording/ transcription</li><li>Coding and analysis can be complex and time-consuming</li></ul>
Focus group	<ul><li>Simple to design</li><li>Useful for gaining in-depth feedback in a short time frame</li><li>Allows for information to be generated by participants (rather than directed by the facilitator)</li></ul>	<ul><li>Requires the availability of a group of appropriate people</li><li>Requires appropriate facilitation (focusing on issues rather than directed questions)</li><li>Requires recording/ transcription</li><li>Coding and analysis can be complex and time-consuming</li></ul>
Questionnaire	<ul><li>Can be simple to design</li><li>Useful for gaining feedback from a number of people</li><li>Easy to administer if you have face-to-face access to respondents</li></ul>	<ul><li>Understanding of survey design is necessary (e.g., use of open-ended versus closed-response questions; avoidance of 'double-barrelled' questions; use of question types that will elicit constructive feedback)</li><li>Responses to online surveys are often low</li><li>The items included may reflect the priorities of the person who designs the survey and miss information that is important to users unless there is consultation during design. Use of appropriate open-ended questions may address this issue to some extent</li></ul>

(Continued)

| Table 5.2 | Comparing some common evaluation methods (*cont'd*) |

Methods	Advantages	Issues to consider
	■ Simple to analyse if checklists, Likert scales or other closed-response question types are used	■ Coding and analysis of open-ended responses can be time-consuming (though these will provide you with richer information than closed-response questions)
Pre- and post-testing	■ Useful for comparing responses before and after implementation of an online innovation	■ Requires decisions about what to include in the tests ■ Difficult to interpret pre- and post-differences: they may be due to a range of factors (not necessarily those under investigation)
Reflection	■ Valuable source of direct experiences (yours or others') ■ Useful for integrating information from all other sources used, and making decisions	■ May be affected by pre-existing beliefs and values – not necessarily reliable and valid ■ May be cumbersome to analyse

question forms as in quizzes but responses are anonymous. Responses to online surveys often tend to be low so you need to think about ways of increasing the rate of return. Think of strategies that you respond to when asked to complete an evaluation. Reminders and repeated requests using a number of different modes (email, online announcements, text messages, requests in class and personal requests) can be effective to increase the response rate. Explaining what and why you are evaluating, and indicating how you intend to respond to the feedback may encourage responses.

■ You can evaluate a discussion forum by looking at its transcript and by manually quantifying response levels to particular tasks.

Although this may be time-consuming, an advantage is that the record of the discussion provides existing documentation for you to interpret.

If you use a reflective cycle to 'process' the results of whatever methods you use at each evaluation phase, and make decisions which will inform the next phase, then the procedure you will follow is illustrated in Figure 5.2.

Using this approach you may work through each cycle several times, usually with increasingly formal evaluation methods. You may evaluate your design thoroughly before moving on to developing your environment. This way you will limit wasted time developing aspects of a design that are not clearly thought out. However, in reality, you will often work through the cycles bit by bit, designing one small part of your environment, developing a prototype of that one part, then going back to the design phase to refine it in the light of what you have discovered in development. At each stage, different methods for evaluation can be used which may include informal conversation, observation, survey, interview, focus groups and so on, as discussed earlier. Regardless of the method, it is necessary to reflect on the evaluation results and identify what they tell you so you can plan the improvements indicated. At the point of reflection you are looking back at the evaluation, and forward to the next planning stage. You will also have the opportunity to reflect on the evaluation itself and its design, and ask questions about its effectiveness and efficiency at indicating needed improvements.

Figure 5.2 A cyclical approach to evaluation during design, development and implementation

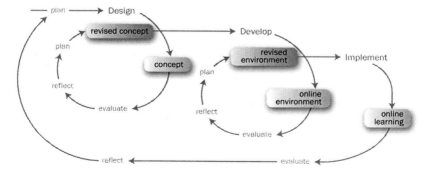

For example ...

You may start by talking with a colleague and eliciting their view on a broad educational design concept. You may then brainstorm ideas for how you might develop the concept before mapping out your ideas. You might then evaluate the plan or design concept by asking colleagues and educational designers to comment on the plan in a number of specific areas.

You can now revise the design concept before moving on to the development phase (the second cycle in Figure 5.2). It is wise to pause and reflect on the evaluation cycle you have completed and ask how well it identified issues and captured ideas. If you are still in doubt over some aspects of the design, or if you received scant feedback, reconsider the evaluation plan (questions, methods). You may benefit from revising the evaluation and going through the cycle again before embarking on the development.

It is advisable to record your initial plan for all phases in an evaluation plan, which we consider in the next section, because this will keep you 'on track' and it may also provide a useful record later for writing up what you did. You can regard this as a 'living' document which you change, if necessary, as you modify your plans.

If you are using reflection as a key component of your evaluation it is also worthwhile keeping a reflective log during design, development and implementation as this will increase the value of your data (it is very easy to forget key issues as you move on to address new ones). If you are asking students or others to provide reflections you should ask them to keep a log too.

For example ...

Use of a blog provides an excellent way of recording reflections for evaluation.

A final but significant point to emphasise before completing this section is the role of your students in evaluation. If your ultimate goal is to improve the learning experiences of your students, you should consider their role in the evaluation very carefully. This does not mean that you need to supply them with more feedback forms, or that the role of other respondents in an evaluation is not important (the role of other respondents will depend on the purpose of the evaluation). What it does mean is that when you are seeking students' experiences of your online environment you should ensure, as far as you can, that the focus is really on their experience, and not yours. Not surprisingly, teaching staff regularly design evaluation forms with items that they think are important but it is quite possible that the focus of students' concerns (both positive and negative) may be on other things. The main point here is that, among the methods you use, make sure that you do address the issue of learner-centredness in your evaluation, though this may involve approaches that are time-consuming from your perspective.

For example ...

- Use of student reflections (as illustrated above) provides an excellent way of evaluating their experience. Student focus groups can be helpful, as long as the focus is on their concerns, and not those of the facilitator.

- Observations of students' behaviour or patterns of usage can be helpful but they may be subject to interpretation. Conclusions based on observation are more likely to be reliable if they are accompanied by students' own explanations of what they are doing.

- Simply talking to students informally may be the easiest approach to manage, as long as there is a systematic way of recording what they say, and as long as the views of the students that you are talking to are likely to be representative of the whole group.

Laurillard's conversational framework can be used as the basis of an evaluation methodology which allows students' perceptions to be fully acknowledged, with data obtained during the learning process analysed phenomenographically and then used to prompt and guide students' explanations during follow-up interviews (Laurillard, 1993).

It is important to recognise, however, that students are often reluctant to participate in evaluations (even offering them a free lunch as an incentive for them to participate in a focus group may not be enough!). This reluctance may be related to repeated requests for their participation in evaluations. To resolve these problems consider your context and circumstances. For example, student representatives who may be on your course management committee are likely to be good sources of information. Otherwise short, informal data collection opportunities may work best. Whatever methods you choose, it is important to close the feedback loop by letting them know what will be/has been done as a result of their feedback so that they can see that their contributions have been valued and their time has not been 'wasted'.

Taking into consideration the evaluation concepts, methods, and the staged approach to evaluation we have covered so far, in the next section we will look at using this, together with additional information, to design your evaluation plan.

Designing your evaluation plan

In this chapter we are focusing on evaluation of an online learning innovation through the design, development and implementation phases, with the ultimate aim of ensuring that the online learning environment is appropriate for enhancing students' learning. However, it is important to recognise that evaluation of aspects of the learning and teaching environment can be undertaken for many different purposes, sometimes involving political and funding reasons far removed from the teaching situation itself. Consequently, evaluation can also be undertaken for many different audiences. The concept of *stakeholders* is important in this. These are the people or bodies with a direct interest in whatever it is you are evaluating. You might think that, in the context of your online development, the only stakeholders would be you and your students. You are certainly the primary stakeholders, but considering the concept more broadly, you would also need to include others in the university responsible for academic or administrative matters or technology support relating to your development, and beyond that to government, and other funding bodies, and so on. This is relevant because when you design your evaluation plan, you need to be very clear about the purpose of your evaluation and the main stakeholders involved.

There are some circumstances when you may need to pay particular attention to including other stakeholders in your evaluation.

> ## For example ...
>
> When you are planning to use the results of the evaluation to support an application for funding your development, or when you are claiming time release from other duties, or your are requesting additional support (such as tutors), or further technology requirements, there will be other key stakeholders who have an interest in your evaluation.

If you are undertaking the evaluation as a formal research project, you will also need to seek ethics approval – check the requirements at your institution. Even when the purpose of evaluation is fairly narrowly defined, there are still a number of decisions to be made and questions to be answered about how the evaluation will be conducted, and it is useful to document these.

Reeves and Hedberg (2003) suggest the following components for a (full) evaluation plan:

- Introduction (covers the major sections of the plan and the primary people involved in writing it).
- Background.
- Purposes (includes all purposes of the evaluation).
- Audiences.
- Decisions (anticipated decisions to be influenced by the evaluation).
- Questions (the evaluation questions to be addressed – as in Table 5.1).
- Method (involves matching options to purposes and questions, and considering budget and timeline).
- Sample (includes rationale for sample sizes).
- Instrumentation (includes all evaluation instruments and tools to be used).
- Limitations (to generalisability and interpretation, including threats to reliability and validity).
- Logistics (outlines who will be responsible for what tasks).
- Timeline (for implementation, analysis and reporting).
- Budget (including personnel time, travel, data preparation such as transcribing, etc.).

When you are planning a simple evaluation that you will undertake primarily yourself, without expectation of any external audience, we suggest that you should still prepare a modified version that includes the items in the left column of Table 5.3, with a view to answering the questions in the right column.

If you are using a questionnaire as an evaluation instrument it will consist of the questions that respondents will answer and rating scales where relevant. Once you have refined a questionnaire that suits your purpose you may use it as an instrument for evaluating other innovations.

This will keep you on track and, if you are intending to use your own reflections for planning the next cycle of development or implementation, will give you a structured way of collecting the evidence that you will need to draw on to make your decisions. Documenting your evaluation plan, together with results, may also have later, unforeseen, benefits.

Table 5.3   **Designing a simple evaluation plan**

Component	Questions to ask yourself
1. Purposes	What are the purposes of this evaluation?
2. Decisions	What decisions will be influenced by this evaluation?
3. Questions	What questions do I need to ask to meet the purposes and help me to make the appropriate decisions?
4. Data sources	Who are the respondents who will give me information to answer the questions and/or what sources do I need to consult?
5. Method	What kind of evaluation design is appropriate to the purposes, questions, timeline and resources?
6. Instrumentation	What evaluation instruments (e.g., questionnaire, rating form, focus group/interview protocol) do I need?
7. Timeline	What timeline do I have available for evaluation during design, development and implementation, and analysis at each stage?
8. Resources	What resources do I need and how will I obtain them?

For example ...

Having this information available will help you if you decide to apply for funding to extend your innovation, or if you want to apply for promotion or a teaching award and need evidence of the value of what you have done, or if you are interested in publishing your results in order to contribute to the scholarship of teaching and learning in higher education (Murray, 2008).

We have discussed the first five components in Table 5.3 and alluded to the last three. There are many evaluation instruments available online which may be useful, either as they are or as a basis for an instrument you develop yourself. In Table 5.1 we referred to evaluation at different stages of design, development and implementation. As part of your evaluation plan you will need to build in a time component to allow this to happen, as well as ensuring you have other resources needed such as computer laboratories or video cameras, depending on the methods you have chosen. You may also need to plan and schedule input from others. This may be important in situations where you are 'too close' to your innovation to be able to run an unbiased evaluation or when you need an independent evaluator for your student cohort. Both these situations have an impact on reliability and validity. You may also need to involve others if you do not have the time or skills to run all aspects of the evaluation yourself.

For example ...

- Do you have skills in survey design? If not, you may need to get assistance in designing a questionnaire.
- Running a focus group yourself with your own students may bias the results if students are reluctant to raise issues that may be seen as critical of you.
- Do you have time to transcribe, analyse and interpret data from interviews or focus groups? If not, you may need to include a budget in your evaluation plan.

Managing, reporting and acting on the evaluation

Managing and reporting

Issues relating to how you will manage and report on your evaluation again depend largely on what your purposes are and the extent to which other stakeholders will be involved. If there are direct implications for audiences other than you and your students, and the evaluation is summative, you (or someone else) will usually also need to prepare a formal evaluation report. Reeves and Hedberg (2003, p. 248) suggest that a typical evaluation report includes:

1. Title.
2. Table of contents.
3. Executive summary.
4. Overview and background (including description of what was evaluated and delineation of the purpose of the evaluation).
5. Decisions (intended to be influenced by the evaluation) and questions (that were addressed).
6. Methodology (including complete description of the design and any instruments that were adapted or developed).
7. Results (possibly organised by methodologies, e.g., interviews, questionnaires, observations, or by the major questions).
8. Recommendations and discussion.
9. References.
10. Appendices.

Owen (2006, p. 20) summarises the findings of an evaluation as:

- *evidence* (the data collected during the evaluation);
- *conclusions* (the interpretations or meanings made through analysis);
- *judgements* (in which values are placed on the conclusions); and
- *recommendations* (the suggested courses of actions in the light of the evidence and conclusions).

Notice how the process of decision-making and judgements about worth, which we considered earlier as key evaluation concepts, are reflected in this summary. Nevertheless, Owen goes on to comment that:

[a]ll evaluative enquiry involves collecting evidence and making conclusions. However, there will be variations from study to study in the degree to which findings incorporate the making of judgments or recommendations.

What form should an evaluation report take?

The traditional evaluation report is a text-based document, as indicated by the components suggested by Reeves and Hedberg above. However, both they and Owen note the use of less traditional forms of reporting. Owen (2006, p. 126) lists the following types of reports:

- written versus oral;
- progress versus final;
- substantive (main report) versus secondary (such as technical details or data management);
- summary versus main report;
- formal versus informal;
- descriptive versus recommendatory.

In referring to non-written reports, he notes that displays and photography/videos may be used and that displays in the form of graphs and charts can summarise and present large amounts of information in an 'attractive' way. He adds that the detail of reporting will vary from evaluation to evaluation and should be negotiated in the planning stage and that generally, a combination of reporting methods is necessary to take into account the needs of different audiences.

These comments are especially relevant for evaluation of online learning environments, and particularly at the design and development stages. Informal reporting may be all that is needed and, because the environment is online, visual reporting that illustrates aspects of the environment and the way that it is used is likely to be highly appropriate.

For example ...

A site map indicating the structure of the online environment and how activities, resources and support are linked will give a broad overview of the experience students will have of the environment.

Acting on the evaluation

Finally, please be aware of the importance of acting on an evaluation. You may wonder why this needs comment if the rationale for undertaking an evaluation is focused on improving the emerging or existing environment to enhance students' learning. However, you might be surprised at how often evaluations are undertaken, and the recommendations are not acted upon. There might be good reasons for this: for example, you may not have the resources to act, or you may consider that some of the recommendations are not appropriate for your students in their current context. If this is the case, then it is important that you explain this to students if they have provided you with some of the data that has led to these recommendations. These situations are probably very unlikely to occur if you have conducted the evaluation yourself and you are using a reflective process to make decisions and judgements about the next phases of planning but they also serve as a reminder not to include items in an evaluation if you do not intend to act on the responses.

Illustrating the ideas in this chapter ...

Suzy continues her story to illustrate how she addressed evaluation of her online environment.

Suzy's story continued ...

I take the quality of my teaching very seriously and reflection is a key concept for me. I try to nurture reflection in the pre-service teachers whom I teach, to support their learning and assessment, and I use it myself to analyse my teaching practice and determine what I will do the same, or differently, next time.

My approach to evaluation is very pragmatic and informal. If I had more time, and didn't have the demands of a young family at home, I would probably be more structured and formal. But as it is, I do action research in my head – I do a lot of thinking about my teaching and I adjust and modify based on my experiences all the time. If there's a problem, I want to know what went wrong and I start thinking through different design and development strategies to work out how I will do it differently next time – evaluation takes the form of troubleshooting. This way of working is an example of reflective practice in action and how professionals often 'think on the job'. The purpose of my informal evaluation activities is always about improvement of the unit by focusing on the way I teach it, while the questions I ask myself are usually about how I could do something better, particularly when I'm aware of a problem.

As a result, evaluation during the design, development and implementation phases tends to merge. This is also partly because I'm the only person teaching this unit and I am using e-learning technologies that I can implement without help so this has contributed to my informal approach – I manage everything myself. However, I'm not alone in this – I talk to my colleagues, I talk to the students, so peer review and obtaining student feedback are part of my formative evaluation strategies too. Building in student reflection on the process of creating the digital responses at the end of their presentations is a vital aspect of evaluation. I also use the tracking system on the LMS to identify which parts of the site are being used most frequently, I observe students in class and note their contributions to discussion on the unit website, and I take their assessment output into consideration as part of my evaluation. So although my evaluation plan isn't written down anywhere, I could easily do that.

The university unit evaluation surveys are the main forms of summative evaluation that I draw on and I find that these give me a really good indication of how students are responding to approaches I have introduced. The ratings from the quantitative items and the qualitative data usually support what my informal formative evaluation strategies have told me. In 2007 I was advised by the Deputy Vice Chancellor (Education) that university survey responses indicated that the unit which included the digital responses was one of the highest performing units in the university.

I also regularly request university evaluations of my teaching which have provided me with teaching and evaluation scores consistently above faculty and university means. Feedback from these formal processes supports the innovations in teaching that I have been introducing and is recognised by the university, and externally. It forms a record of achievement that I can use in applications for teaching awards and obviates the need for other evaluation reports.

Summary

In this chapter we have covered some evaluation concepts, processes and issues that may be useful as you plan, develop and implement your online environment. We have suggested that valuable concepts include the idea that evaluation involves decisions about the worth of something, using a cyclical, iterative process with reflection as an important component which can form the major strategy for 'processing' information from other strategies when making decisions. We have supported a pragmatic, eclectic approach to evaluation, emphasising its importance during design, development and implementation, using simple strategies to encompass both formative and summative evaluation.

We have also emphasised that the purposes of the evaluation should be your starting point, recognising that evaluations can be undertaken for many different purposes and that there is a range of stakeholders who may have an interest in your evaluation. We have suggested that it is worthwhile preparing a simple evaluation plan even if your purposes are quite narrow and you consider that the main stakeholders are you and your students. It is this plan that will identify the evaluation questions you need to ask to meet the purposes, the data sources that will provide the information, the most appropriate methods to use, and the resources you will require. If the purpose of your evaluation is related to the improvement of student learning, make sure that you include strategies that will authentically capture their experiences. Remember, too, that you can include information from other sources (such as university evaluations) as part of your plan. Finally, we have noted some ideas about managing, reporting and acting on your evaluation that we suggest you should consider.

Following we continue the checklist which you began in Chapter 1. The section here covers the aspects of evaluation we have addressed in this chapter. As before, if you are able to answer 'Yes' to most questions, you should have a good sense of what is involved, in this case with evaluating your online environment. If your answer to most questions is 'No', we suggest that you take the advice we suggested previously in relation to online design, and start with something small and simple. Perhaps try and think of one easy evaluation method that you could implement at each of the stages of design, development and evaluation – keeping in mind that talking to colleagues, talking to students, recording your own reflections, using the LMS tracking system, and so on, all count as evaluation methods in this context.

Are you able to identify ...	Yes	Unsure	No
31. The concepts that will help to guide the evaluation of your online learning environment?			
32. The kinds of purposes and questions that might guide your evaluation during design, development and implementation?			
33. The evaluation methods you might use to meet the above purposes and answer the questions?			
34. How you might design your evaluation plan?			
35. How you would deal with managing, reporting and acting on the evaluation?			
36. Any other factors that you may need to consider in evaluating your online environment? (Specify below.)			

6

Conclusion

Introduction

We will briefly review the main ideas that have contributed to this guide and then consider the future, addressing questions such as:

- Once you have been through your first cycle of online teaching and assessment, what is the next step?
- How will you accommodate emerging technologies when you do not know what affordances they might offer?

Very broadly, the first question can be addressed by using the cyclical approach to evaluation we considered in Chapter 5. The answer to the second question relates to a statement we made at the beginning of the book: *You do not need to be unnerved by the volatility of the educational technology landscape as the principles informing this framework are much less subject to change than the technologies themselves*. Because the planning framework is built on pedagogical rather than technological foundations, it should help you to accommodate new technologies, and new ways of teaching, as they emerge, even though you do not know yet what these will be.

We will explore these ideas further in the sections that follow. At the end of this chapter we have put together the checklist that we have built up with you over the last five chapters so that you can copy it and use it in its complete form if you wish.

Introducing online learning and assessment – a brief review

We began with the assumption that you are new to teaching or assessing with technology but are interested in its potential to enhance your students' learning. We also assumed that you might be taking this step largely on your own, using resources that are available to you, rather than being a member of a project team undertaking a major new initiative. With those assumptions in mind, we commented that where you need to start if you are thinking about introducing technology into your teaching or assessment is really in the same place that you would start if you were planning any new teaching activity. We will now briefly summarise the main steps that we suggested you follow to plan and implement your innovation so that you are in a position to refine it during subsequent iterations.

If you begin by considering your views about how students learn, in the context of the two major learning theories which have influenced the fields of higher education and educational technology (phenomenography and constructivism), your focus will be on the active involvement of your students in the learning process. Thinking about how they learn, along with the nature of good teaching in higher education, the characteristics of your students, your characteristics as a teacher, and your learning and teaching context, will set the scene for planning online learning and assessment. Then, if you begin with an issue, problem or opportunity related to the learning of your students which allows you to recognise some learning objectives that they might be able to meet online, you will be ready to start reconceptualising your teaching in the online environment.

Keeping your focus on the learning objectives you have identified will allow you to determine the affordances of the technologies you will require. We also suggested that you consider your institution's policies and infrastructure relating to online learning and assessment because of the administrative and support benefits of using institutional systems. In Chapter 2 we described the features of the main technologies currently available for online teaching and assessment so that you could consider your requirements, and your context, against these characteristics. To finalise your technology selection you need to be aware of, and have strategies for dealing with, some of the common student support, management and administrative issues that you might face.

At this point you should be ready to begin your online learning design and development. These processes will be influenced by whether you are planning online learning or assessment which will take place in a classroom setting, in a blended environment, or fully online. The concepts of transactional distance and transactional control are two additional theoretical perspectives which might assist you, and there are a number of online learning models that can be used to guide design. We focused particularly on Oliver and Herrington's (2001) constructivist model which provides a simple way of conceptualising how learning activities, resources and supports may be designed and related to assessment. We also noted the concept of constructively aligning learning objectives, activities and assessment (and the advantage of merging authentic learning activities and assessment), before considering some common types of learning activities that involve interaction between users (discussion activities and others), interaction with content, and creation of content. We briefly noted some issues that you may face in developing your design and suggested some additional general student support issues, as well as management and administrative issues that you might need to consider in implementing your design.

If you are planning to assess in the online environment, we suggested that you take into consideration current views about the nature and purpose of assessment in higher education which focus on its role in learning. This will give you ideas for thinking about formative and summative assessment in the online environment. It will also be helpful in considering options for determining who undertakes assessment (including self, peer and group assessment), and the assessment design principles that will guide your planning. It is likely that your planning will involve one or more of the four major uses of the online environment for assessment (online submission, automated assessment, online discussion and web publishing), and we have suggested some of the opportunities and challenges related to each. Moving through these uses tends to offer increasing opportunities for taking advantage of the online environment to reconceptualise assessment tasks, rather than simply transposing existing tasks. Again, there is a range of student support issues and management and administrative issues, that you may need to consider, particularly if you are planning time-limited summative assessment tasks that are not undertaken in computer laboratories.

Finally, we addressed the important role of evaluation in monitoring the quality of your online environment, emphasising the use of a simple, eclectic, pragmatic approach that highlights the role of reflection in a continuous cycle of iterative, learner-centred improvement through design, development and implementation. Preparing an evaluation plan based on the purpose/s of the evaluation will determine the questions you need to ask, the data sources and methods you will use to answer those questions, and the resources you will need to conduct the evaluation. There are also a number of issues that you may need to consider in relation to managing, reporting and acting on your evaluation.

The above stages provide a learner-centred framework that you can follow, whatever your starting point, whatever the resources available to you, and irrespective of whether you are using a classroom-enhanced, blended or fully online environment extending to off-campus or transnational teaching. As we have noted several times throughout the book, it is best to start small if you can, although we recognise that sometimes institutional imperatives to 'get your subject online' do not make this possible, and that these same pressures may also sometimes compromise the quality of what is offered on online. Nevertheless, it is advisable to be as well-prepared as you can.

Accommodating emerging technologies

There are three main reasons that this framework can continue to guide your planning into the future, helping you to accommodate technologies that may not have emerged yet, or that you are not yet familiar with. We have mentioned all of these previously but we will expand on them here.

- The framework is based on pedagogical principles that are much less volatile than recent changes in technology, and therefore their use provides a consistent way of approaching these changes.

For example ...

- The learning objectives that you hope your students will achieve are likely to be informed by learning and teaching principles that are valued in higher education. These principles will guide you when you consider new technologies to look for ways they might be implemented (as we saw in Chapter 2).
- The affordances of new technologies often give new impetus to learning theories that pre-date them, as has happened with social constructivism.

We need to recognise, of course, that theories about what is valuable in learning do change over time (as we noted in relation to behaviourism in Chapter 1), but the main point here is that these changes occur much more slowly than changes in technologies. It is also important to acknowledge that affordance of emerging technologies may offer ways of teaching that you have not yet considered. These teaching strategies are still likely to be consistent with existing learning theories, but it is possible that they might challenge them.

For example ...

Although the importance of student-centredness in learning is supported by a number of longstanding learning theories, this is usually accompanied by an assumption that the teacher will nevertheless control the planning of the student-centred environment. The affordances of Web 2.0 applications, with their potential for social engagement and learner control, may be seen as challenging assumptions about the control of teachers and the control of knowledge.

■ Secondly, the evaluation approach that we have suggested offers an intrinsic capacity for ongoing improvement via iterative, incremental steps, which are responsive to the complexities of the environments in which learning takes place. It provides for continual adjustment to specific circumstances and student cohorts, while the reflective process allows you to bring together information from a range of other strategies during design, development and implementation, providing for a considered and comprehensive decision-making process. Using this process you can gradually accommodate new technologies into your teaching, to an extent, and at a pace which fits your context.

For example ...

You might begin a student group project which involves discussion and preparation of a group report by using a discussion space within your LMS, with students circulating drafts of the report as attachments. You might move on from this to using a wiki, once you feel comfortable in supporting them in that environment, because of the benefits we have discussed previously which include the availability of a single web-based document for them to work on.

- Thirdly, the time lag between the emergence of a new technology and its availability as a university-supported system works to your advantage, giving you time to:
  - identify whether its affordances are appropriate to your learning and teaching context, and, if so, to plan how you might implement it;
  - determine whether it is stable enough to use for teaching or assessment; or
  - establish whether it is just a passing fad.

For example ...

Second Life has potential for learning but in early versions mobility was hard to manage and an inexperienced user could spend hours with their avatar 'stuck' in a particular room. Time, experience, improvements in the software, as well as consideration of student characteristics, contextual factors and the learning objectives are required to determine the costs and benefits of using environments such as these.

As you become more comfortable with teaching online you may sometimes want to move ahead of institutional systems and by that stage you should be fully aware of the implications of doing that and be able to manage it successfully.

Illustrating the ideas in this chapter ...

Finally, Suzy concludes her story and comments on her plans for the future.

Suzy's story – where to from here?

Involvement of students in the preparation of digital responses has been just one of the online teaching approaches I have used. However, this use of the online environment has been important in helping me to crystallise my ideas on learning through assessment.

I plan to continue to develop this idea, and to apply it in different ways in my teaching, because it has such a powerful impact on students' learning. In relating theory and practice through this authentic assessment task, students are also developing a number of professional attributes, including independence, team work and the ability to think critically and reflectively.

In another unit I am using the online environment to encourage students to be researchers, inducting them into the skills necessary to find the research literature relevant to the professional challenges they will face as practising educators. I have made a deliberate decision to make the processes behind research explicit to students, and to teach them what databases are, how databases work, and how to locate current and relevant literature for their assignments. I undertake this process with a large cohort (n = 195) of first year students by explaining how peer review works, the importance of peer review to the academic community and problems associated with simply Googling topics and citing any given website in an assignment. This process has been framed by an assessed task in which students develop an educational resource, and then conduct peer reviews of each other's work. Students are required to develop the criteria they will use to conduct the review, and then submit the review as their first assignment. Completed reviews are handed back to the original authors of the resources and the resources are then amended in line with the reviewer feedback and submitted for assessment as the final assignment. In this unit of study, resources I have made available to the students include sample reviewer guidelines from journals for which I have conducted reviews, and examples of reviewer feedback I have received about my own work. Participating in the peer review process as the basis for assessment and having access to real examples of reviewer feedback has meant the students are more able to understand the process involved in the generation of research and know what is actually meant by the term 'peer reviewed'.

Students value this experience, noting that they had previously been unable to fully access academic support services as they had no existing conception of peer review, or of the difference between journals, journal articles, books and book chapters. The explicit teaching of these key academic literacy skills produces outcomes that allow students to engage in quality independent study and to critique the reliability and validity of the information they cite in their assignments. However, university evaluations of this unit have not been quite as high as they have for other innovations I have introduced so I am keen to investigate the reasons for this.

I have recently begun to explore the possibilities of Web 2.0 applications and can see the potential for supporting reflection and communication, as well as streamlining collaborative group work, by avoiding the rather cumbersome process of working with discussion messages and attachments. There are many challenges, as emerging technologies continue to push the boundaries of possibilities for creating learning activities that help students to develop reflective perspectives on the theory/practice relationship and demonstrate their emerging abilities as pre-service teachers. However, these emerging possibilities offer an exciting catalyst to my own reflection about teaching, offering tools and strategies to explore new dimensions of active learning.

Summary

We have now reached the end of this planning guide for introducing online learning and assessment. If you follow the ideas in this guide, the end of planning and development for you will be implementation and the potential of many new beginnings as you refine your ideas and move forward into an ongoing cycle of improvement based on experience and evaluation.

In this chapter we have reviewed the planning stages covered in Chapters 1 to 5, moving through the process you might follow if you have no experience of online teaching or assessment but are interested in their potential to improve your students' learning. We have assumed that you are responsible for teaching a particular subject or course and that you are working primarily as an individual, using systems and resources easily available to you. Large and complex online learning projects usually cannot be achieved at this level because they may require a team of people with different skills (for example, an educational designer, a web developer, a multimedia developer, a graphic designer, audiovisual staff), and considerable funding, and project management expertise to bring them to fruition.

We have explained why this planning framework is applicable whatever new opportunities for teaching with technology may emerge because it is based on pedagogical principles that are unlikely to undergo rapid change, because the suggested evaluation approach has an intrinsic capacity for ongoing improvement, and because you can take advantage of the time lag between the availability of emerging technologies and their uptake by universities, to explore whether and how you might be able to use them to help students meet specific learning objectives.

Following is the complete version of the checklist which you began in Chapter 1. Check your totals for each column to assess your readiness to begin. If you answer 'Yes' to about three-quarters of the questions, you are probably ready to proceed with your planning without too much difficulty. The number of answers in the 'Unsure' and 'No' columns will give you some idea of the extent of further assistance you may need to seek. Also check any of the five areas where your 'Yes', 'Unsure' and 'No' responses are dominant, as this will indicate your strengths or requirements for support in particular areas.

This book has provided an overview of the steps involved in preparing for pedagogically-effective online learning and assessment. While its scope does not extend to detailed advice on development and implementation, it is intended as a guide that will help you in your initial planning. Your enthusiasm for good teaching is the most important factor in your success. Interest in your students and their learning, along with passion and curiosity about your subject, will lead you to seek effective ways of teaching which provide the best foundation for using new technologies in interesting ways. All the technology in the world won't *make* you a good teacher but wise use of it may make teaching and learning easier, more engaging, more effective, and maybe more fun.

Introducing online learning and assessment – a planning guide

Are you able to identify ...	Yes	Unsure	No
Where to start (Chapter 1)			
1. Your views on how your students learn (preferably as they relate to one or more contemporary learning theories)?			
2. Your position in relation to current views about the nature of good teaching in higher education?			
3. The characteristics of your students that may be important for online learning or assessment?			
4. Your characteristics as a teacher that may be important for online teaching or assessment?			
5. Aspects of both the learning context and your teaching context that may be important for online teaching or assessment?			
6. An issue, problem or opportunity related to the learning or assessment of your students that allows you to recognise one or more learning objectives that they may be able to meet online?			
7. How the transition to online learning or assessment may require you to reconceptualise your teaching?			
8. Any other factors that may encourage you to consider online learning or assessment? (Specify below.)			

Are you able to identify ...	Yes	Unsure	No
Teaching with technology – considering your options (Chapter 2)			
9. Some technologies which offer the affordances that will allow students to meet online the learning objectives you have identified?			
10. How your institution's policies and infrastructure will affect the technologies you choose?			
11. The specific technologies that you will select for online learning or assessment?			
12. The support that your students might need in order to use these technologies, and how this support will be provided?			
13. The management and administrative issues that you need to deal with as you begin to teach or assess using these technologies, and strategies for dealing with them?			
14. Any other factors that you may need to consider in deciding your technology options? (Specify below.)			
Online learning design and development (Chapter 3)			
15. Any additional theories or models that will help to guide your online learning design?			
16. How you will align the objectives that are driving your online learning design with appropriate learning activities and assessment tasks?			

Are you able to identify ...	Yes	Unsure	No
17. The kinds of activities that you will design involving interaction between users, interaction with content and/or creation of content?			
18. The kinds of specific learning resources and supports that you will need to design for the activities you plan to develop?			
19. Issues that you may face in developing your design and how you will address them?			
20. General student support issues you will need to consider in designing your environment and how you will address them?			
21. The management and administrative issues that you may need to deal with as you begin to implement specific aspects of your design (e.g., online discussion groups or Web 2.0 spaces such as blogs or wikis), and strategies for dealing with them?			
22. Any other factors that you may need to consider in designing or developing your online environment? (Specify below.)			
Online assessment (Chapter 4)			
23. Your view of the nature and purposes of assessment which will guide you in your online assessment design?			
24. Your answer to the question of 'Who assesses?' and how you might implement this online?			

Are you able to identify ...	Yes	Unsure	No
25. Some principles that will guide you in your online assessment design?			
26. The uses that you will make of the online environment for assessment?			
27. Some of the opportunities and challenges associated with the uses of the online environment you have chosen?			
28. The student support issues relating to online assessment which you may need to consider?			
29. The management and administrative issues relating to online assessment which you may need to consider (and which you could summarise in a risk analysis)?			
30. Any other factors that you may need to consider in designing your online assessment? (Specify below.)			
Evaluation (Chapter 5)			
31. The concepts that will help to guide the evaluation of your online learning environment?			
32. The kinds of purposes and questions that might guide your evaluation during design, development and implementation?			

Are you able to identify ...	Yes	Unsure	No
33. The evaluation methods you might use to meet the above purposes and answer the questions?			
34. How you might design your evaluation plan?			
35. How you would deal with managing reporting and acting on the evaluation? higher education?			
36. Any other factors that you may need to consider in evaluating your online environment? (Specify below.)			
TOTAL			

References

Alexander, S., & Hedberg, J. G. (1994). Evaluating technology-based learning: Which model? In K. Beattie, C. McNaught & S. Wills (Eds.), *Interactive multimedia in university education: Designing for change in teaching and learning* (pp. 233–44). Amsterdam: Elsevier.

Allen, C. (2004). *Tracing the evolution of social software.* Retrieved 20 January 2010 from *http://www.lifewithalacrity.com/2004/10/tracing_the_evo.html*

Amory, A. (2007). Game object model version II: A theoretical framework for educational game development. *Educational Technology Research and Development, 15*, 51–77.

Anderson, L., Krathwohl, D. R., Airasian, P. W., Cruikshank, K. A., Mayer, R. E., Pintrich, P. R., . . . Wittrock, M.C. (Eds.) (2001). *A taxonomy for learning, teaching, and assessing: A revision of Bloom's taxonomy of educational objectives.* New York: Longman.

Aubusson, P., Schuck, S., & Burden, K. (2009). Mobile learning for teacher professional learning: Benefits, obstacles and issues. *ALT-J, 17*(3), 233–47.

Bain, J. (1999). Introduction: Learning-centred evaluation of innovation in higher education. *Higher Education Research and Development, 18*(2), 165–72.

Barnes, C., & Tynan, B. (2007). The adventures of Miranda in the brave new world: Learning in a Web 2.0 millennium. *ALT-J, 15*(3), 189–200.

Bates A. W. (2005). *Technology, e-learning and distance education.* London: RoutledgeFalmer.

Bennett, S., Maton, K., & Kervin, L. (2008). The 'digital natives' debate: A critical review of the evidence. *British Journal of Educational Technology, 39*(5), 775–86.

Benson, R., & Brack, C. (2009). Developing the scholarship of teaching: What is the role of e-teaching and learning? *Teaching in Higher Education, 14*(1), 71–80.

Benson, R., & Samarawickrema, G. (2009). Addressing the context of e-learning: Using transactional distance theory to inform design. *Distance Education, 30*(1), 5–21.

Biggs, J., & Tang, C. (2007). *Teaching for quality learning at university* (3rd ed.). Maidenhead: SRHE & Open University Press.

Boud, D. (1991). *Implementing student self assessment* (HERDSA Green Guide No. 5). Kensington, NSW: HERDSA.

Boud, D. (1995). Assessment and learning: Contradictory or complementary? In P. Knight (Ed.), *Assessment for learning in higher education* (pp. 35–48). London: Kogan Page.

Boud, D. (2007). Reframing assessment as if learning were important. In D. Boud & N. Falchikov (Eds.), *Rethinking assessment in higher education: Learning for the longer term* (pp. 14–25). London: Routledge.

Boud, D., & Falchikov, N. (2006). Aligning assessment with long-term learning. *Assessment & Evaluation in Higher Education, 31*(4), 399–413.

Brew, A. (2006) *Research and teaching: Beyond the divide.* Houndmills, UK: Palgrave MacMillan.

Carless, D. (2007). Learning-oriented assessment: Conceptual bases and practical implications. *Innovations in Education and Teaching International, 44*(1), 57–66.

Chickering, A. W., & Gamson, Z. F. (1987). Seven principles for good practice in undergraduate education. *American Association of Higher Education Bulletin, 39*(7), 3–7.

Crooks, T. (1988). *Assessing student performance* (HERDSA Green Guide No. 8). Kensington, NSW: HERDSA.

Dewey, J. (1963). *Experience and education.* New York: Collier (original work published 1938).

Dron, J. (2007a). *Control and constraint in e-learning: Choosing when to choose.* Hershey, PA: Information Science Publishing.

Dron, J. (2007b). Designing the undesignable: Social software and control. *Educational Technology & Society, 10*(3), 60–71. *http://www.ifets.info/journals/10_3/5.pdf*

Duffy, T. M., & Jonassen, D. H. (1992). Constructivism: New implications for instructional technology. In T. M. Duffy & D. H. Jonassen (Eds.), *Constructivism and the technology of instruction* (pp. 1–16). Hillsdale, NJ: Lawrence Erlbaum.

Earl, L. M. (2003). *Assessment as learning: Using classroom assessment to maximize student learning.* Thousand Oaks, CA: Corwin Press.

Falchikov, N. (2005). *Improving assessment through student involvement.* London: RoutledgeFalmer.

Garrison, D.R., & Anderson, T. (2003). *E-learning in the 21st century* (pp. 22–31). London: Routledge.

Garrison, D. R., & Kanuka, H. (2004). Blended learning: Uncovering its transformative potential in higher education. *The Internet and Higher Education, 7*, 95–105.

Gibbs, G., Habeshaw, S. & Habeshaw, T. (1988). *53 Interesting ways to assess your students.* Bristol: Technical and Educational Services Ltd.

Grabinger, R. S. (1996). Rich environments for active learning. In D. H. Jonassen (Ed.), *Handbook of research for educational communications and technology* (pp. 665–92). New York: Macmillan.

Harvey, J. (1998). *Evaluation Cookbook.* Edinburgh: Learning Technology Dissemination Initiative. Retrieved 20 January 2010 from *http://www.icbl.hw.ac.uk/ltdi/cookbook/*

James, R., McInnis, C., & Devlin, M. (2002). *Assessing learning in Australian universities.* Melbourne: Centre for the Study of Higher Education and The Australian Universities Teaching Committee. Retrieved 20 January 2010 from *http://www.cshe.unimelb.edu.au/assessinglearning/docs/AssessingLearning.pdf*

Jonassen, D. H. (1991). Objectivism vs constructivism: Do we need a philosophical paradigm shift? *Educational Technology Research and Development, 39*(3), 5–14.

Jones, G., Edwards, G., & Reid, A. (2009). How can mobile SMS communication support and enhance a first year undergraduate learning environment? *ALT-J, 17*(3), 201–18.

Kember, D. (2000). *Action learning and action research: Improving the quality of teaching and learning*. London: RoutledgeFalmer.

Kennedy, G., Dalgarno, B., Bennett, S., Gray, K., Waycott, J., Judd, T., . . . Chang, R. (2009). *Educating the net generation: A handbook of findings for practice and policy*. Retrieved 20 January 2010 from *http://www.netgen.unimelb.edu. au/downloads/handbook/NetGenHandbookAll.pdf*

Kennedy, G. J. (2005). Peer-assessment in group projects: Is it worth it? In A. Young & D. Tolhurst (Eds.), *Conferences in Research in Practice in Information Technology, Vol. 42*. Retrieved 20 January 2010 from *http://crpit.com/ confpapers/CRPITV42Kennedy.pdf*

Knight, P. (2006). The local practices of assessment. *Assessment & Evaluation in Higher Education, 31*(4), 435–52.

Knight, P., & Yorke, M. (2004). *Learning, curriculum and employability in higher education*. London: RoutledgeFalmer.

Kravtsov, G. G., & Kravtsova, E. E. (2009). Cultural-historical psychology in the practice of education. In M. Fleer, M. Hedegaard & J. Tudge (Eds.), *Childhood studies and the impact of globalization: Policies and practices at global and local levels* (pp. 202–12). New York: Routledge.

Laurillard, D. (1993). *Rethinking university teaching: A framework for the effective use of educational technology*. London: Routledge.

Laurillard, D. (2002). *Rethinking university teaching: A conversational framework for the effective use of learning technologies* (2nd ed.). London: Routledge.

Laurillard, D. (2008). The teacher as action researcher: Using technology to capture pedagogic form. *Studies in Higher Education, 33*(2), 139–54.

Li, L. K. Y. (2001). Some refinements on peer assessment of group projects. *Assessment & Evaluation in Higher Education, 26*(1), 5–18.

Marsh, H. W. (2007). Students' evaluation of university teaching: Dimensionality, reliability, validity, potential biases and usefulness. In R. P. Perry & J. C. Smart (Eds.), *The scholarship of teaching and learning in higher education: An evidence-based perspective* (pp. 319–83). Dordrecht: Springer.

Marton, F., & Booth, S. (1997). *Learning and awareness*. Mahwah, NJ: Lawrence Erlbaum.

Mason, R., & Kaye, A. (Eds.) (1989). *Mindweave: Communication, computers and distance education*. Oxford: Pergamon.

Mathur, S., & Murray, T. (2006). Authentic assessment online: A practical and theoretical challenge in higher education. In D. D. Williams, S. L. Howell & M. Hricko (Eds.), *Online assessment, measurement and evaluation: Emerging practices* (pp. 238–58). Hershey, PA: Information Science Publishing.

Middleton, A. (2009). Beyond podcasting: Creative approaches to designing educational audio. *ALT-J, 17*(2), 143–55.

Moore, M. (1993). Theory of transactional distance. In D. Keegan (Ed.), *Theoretical principles of distance education* (pp. 22–38). Routledge: London.

Moore, M. (2004). Constructivists: Don't blame the tools! *The American Journal of Distance Education, 18*(2), 67–72.

Moore, M. G. (2007). The theory of transactional distance. In M. G. Moore (Ed.), *Handbook of distance education* (pp. 89–105) (2nd ed.). Mahwah, NJ: Lawrence Erlbaum Associates.

Murray, R. (Ed.) (2008) *The scholarship of teaching and learning in higher education*. Maidenhead: SRHE and Open University Press.

Nichols, M. (2008). Institutional perspectives: The challenges of e-learning diffusion. *British Journal of Educational Technology, 39*(4), 598–609.

Nicol, D. J., & Macfarlane-Dick, D. (2006). Formative assessment and self-regulated learning: A model and seven principles of good feedback practice. *Studies in Higher Education, 31*(2), 199–218.

Oliver, R. (2000). When teaching meets learning: Design principles and strategies for web-based learning environments that support knowledge construction. In R. Sims, M. O'Reilly & S. Sawkins (Eds.), *Learning to choose: Choosing to learn. Proceedings of the 17th Annual ASCILITE Conference* (pp. 17–28). Lismore: Southern Cross University Press.

Oliver, R. & Herrington, J. (2001). *Teaching and learning online: A beginner's guide to e-learning and e-teaching in higher education*. Mt Lawley, WA: Centre for Research in Information Technology and Communication, Edith Cowan University. *http://industry.flexiblelearning.net.au/Guide/Resources/Oliver_Herrington.pdf*

O'Reilly, T. (2005). *What is Web 2.0: Design patterns and business models for the next generation of software*. Retrieved 20 January 2010 from *http://www.oreillynet.com/pub/a/oreilly/tim/news/2005/09/30/what-is-web-20.html*

Owen, J. M. (2006). *Program evaluation: Forms and approaches*. Crows Nest, NSW: Allen & Unwin.

Panko, M. (2006). Learning and assessment: A case study – going the full Monty. In T. S. Roberts (Ed.), *Self, peer and group assessment in e-learning* (pp. 85–100). Hershey, PA: Information Science Publishing.

Parlett, M., & Hamilton, D. (1977). Evaluation as illumination: A new approach to the study of innovatory programmes. In D. Hamilton, D. Jenkins, C. King, B. MacDonald & M. Parlett (Eds.), *Beyond the numbers game: A reader in educational evaluation* (pp. 6–22). Basingstoke: Macmillan.

Phillips, R., Bain, J., McNaught, C., Rice, M., & Tripp, D. (2000). *Handbook for learning centred evaluation of computer facilitated learning projects in higher education*. Perth: Murdoch University and ASCILITE.

Prensky, M. (2001) Digital natives, digital immigrants. *On the Horizon, 9*(5). Retrieved 20 January 2010 from *http://www.marprensky.com/writing/Prensky%20-%20Digital%20Natives,%20Digital%20Immigrants%20-%20Part1.pdf*

Raban, R., & Litchfield, A. (2007). Supporting peer assessment of individual contributions in groupwork. *Australasian Journal of Educational Technology, 23*(1), 34–47.

Ramsden, P. (2003). *Learning to teach in higher education* (2nd ed.). London: RoutledgeFalmer.

Reeves, B., Malone, T. W., & O'Driscoll, T. (2008). Leadership's online labs. *Harvard Business Review*, May, 59–66.

Reeves, T. C., & Hedberg, J. G. (2003). *Interactive learning systems evaluation*. Englewood Cliffs, NJ: Educational Technology Publications.

Richardson, J. T. E. (1999). The concepts and methods of phenomenographic research. *Review of Educational Research, 69*(1), 53–82.

Richardson, W. (2009). *Blogs, wikis, podcasts, and other powerful web tools for classrooms* (2nd ed.). Thousand Oaks, CA: Corwin Press.

Roberts, T. S. (2006). Self, peer and group assessment in e-learning: An introduction. In T. S. Roberts (Ed.), *Self, peer and group assessment in e-learning* (pp. 1–16). Hershey, PA: Information Science Publishing.

Rogers, E. M. (2003). *Diffusion of innovations* (5th ed.). New York: The Free Press.

Rowntree, D. (1977). *Assessing students: How shall we know them?* London: Harper & Row.

Salmon, G. (2002). *E-tivities: The key to active online learning.* London: Kogan Page.

Salmon, G. (2003). *E-moderating: The key to teaching and learning online* (2nd ed.). London: RoutledgeFalmer.

Schön, D. A. (1983). *The reflective practitioner: How professionals think in action.* Aldershot: Ashgate.

Schön, D. A. (1987). *Educating the reflective practitioner.* San Francisco: Jossey-Bass.

Schön, D. (1995) The new scholarship requires a new epistemology, *Change*, 27(6), 26–34.

Scriven, M. (1967). The methodology of evaluation. In R. W. Tyler, R. M. Gagné & M. Scriven (Eds.), *Perspectives of curriculum evaluation* (pp. 39–83). Chicago, IL: Rand McNally.

Serafini, F. (2004). Three paradigms of assessment: Measurement, procedure, and inquiry. In International Reading Association (Ed.), *Preparing reading professionals* (pp. 207–16). Newark, DE: International Reading Association.

Sharples, M. (Ed.) (2007). *Big issues in mobile learning. Report of a workshop by the Kaleidoscope Network of Excellence Mobile Learning Initiative.* Nottingham, UK: University of Nottingham, Learning Sciences Research Institute.

Shirky, C. (2003). A group is its own worst enemy. Retrieved 20 January 2010 from *http://shirky.com/writings/group_enemy.html*

Sims, R. (1999). Interactivity on stage: Strategies for learner-designer communication. *Australian Journal of Educational Technology*, 15(3), 257–72.

Squire, K. (2006). From content to context: Video games as designed experience. *Educational Researcher*, 35(8), 19–29.

Stufflebeam, D. L. (1972). The relevance of the CIPP evaluation model for educational accountability. *SRIS Quarterly*, 5(1).

Sung, Y.-T., Chang, K.-E., Chiou, S.-K., & Hou, H.-T. (2005). The design and application of a web-based self- and peer-assessment system. *Computers & Education*, 45, 187–92.

The Pennsylvania State University (2007). Types of questions for on-line discussion. *Penn State learning design community hub.* Retrieved 20 January 2010 from *http://ets.tlt.psu.edu/learningdesign/crafting_question/quest_types*

The TLT Group (2009). Flashlight Program. Evaluation. Assessment. Action. Retrieved 20 January 2010 from *http://www.tltgroup.org/flashlightP.htm*

Thompson, L. (2007). Podcasting: The ultimate learning experience and authentic assessment. In R. J. Atkinson, C. McBeath, S. K. A. Soong & C. Cheers (Eds.), *ICT: Providing choices for learners and learning. Proceedings ascilite Singapore 2007* (pp. 1019–23). Singapore: Centre for Educational Development, Nanyang Technological University. Retrieved 20 January 2010 from *http://www.ascilite.org.au/conferences/singapore07/procs/thompson-poster.pdf*

Tucker, R., Fermelis, J., & Palmer, S. (2009). Designing, implementing and evaluating a Self-and-Peer Assessment tool for e-learning environments. In C. Spratt & P. Lajbcygier (Eds.), *E-learning technologies and evidence-based assessment approaches* (pp. 170–94). Hershey, PA: Information Science Publishing.

Vygotsky, L. (1978). *Mind in society: The development of higher psychological processes*. Cambridge, MA: Harvard University Press.

Index

3

CPSIA information can be obtained at www.ICGtesting.com
Printed in the USA
BVOW04s0634030813

327695BV00001B/17/P